The Secrets of Successful

Practising for Guitarists

This book is dedicated to my family, Eileen, Corena and Tania, for understanding why I had to practise.

Also to my parents Elsie and (the late) Jim, who are still wondering when I will get a real job.

Special thanks to Sharmian Firth and the staff of Dunmore Press who made the production of this book seem so easy.

The Secrets of Successful Practising for Guitarists

By Kevin Downing

© 2000 Kevin Downing
© 2000 Dunmore Press Limited

First published in 2000
by Dunmore Press Ltd
P.O. Box 5115
Palmerston North
New Zealand
http://www.dunmore.co.nz

Australian Supplier:
Federation Press
P.O. Box 45
Annandale 2038 NSW
Australia
Ph: (02) 9552-2200
Fax: (02) 9552-1681

ISBN 0 86469 377 X

Text: Future Bk Bt 12/14
Printer: The Dunmore Printing Company Ltd
               Palmerston North
Cover Design: Stephanie Milne

Contents

How to Use This Book

This book is not one to read once, put on your bookshelf, and then forget. I suggest you read it through the first time, take one or two important points, and put them into practice immediately. In about six to eight weeks, read it again and add a few more points to your practice schedule. Re-read until you have everything mentioned in this book in your practice schedule.

As you read through the book you will come across some familiar ideas. Try to expand on them if you can. As you implement these ideas you will think of others. You could write them down on the blank parts of the page, in a separate notebook or use the blank pages at the end of this book.

The ideas begin with the easiest and progress through to the more advanced. In certain parts of the book I repeat things that I've mentioned in earlier chapters. This is because I think they are so important that you need reminding about them.

This book is similar to a scale book in that you can use it for reference once you have worked from it. For example, if you cannot remember the C major scale, just look it up in the scale book and there you have it. With this book if you are ever unsure about how to practise in the most effective manner, just refer to the section you need and you will save yourself a lot of time and frustration. I only wish there had been a book like this available when I was beginning.

A Special Note for Teachers

This book is written in plain language so that any student can understand it. I recommend that students have their own copy to refer to. The benefits of this are that they will be happy practising independently, and will produce better quality work.

Reading through the book with your students could be beneficial, and you could add some of your own ideas to each chapter as you read.

I would appreciate any comments that you might have regarding this book or subject. My contact address is at the end of the book.

Introduction

There are millions of guitars sold each year, and many millions of people already own one, but most of the time these guitars remain underneath a bed or in a closet. Their owners have become frustrated and given up, most often because they have never developed a good practice system. And even people who do practise on a regular basis are not sure they are doing it properly.

Looking back over our school and university years, study at home was considered really important, but ironically most of us were never taught how to study. You may recall that some people in your class were always top students, and others were always struggling. The top students knew the simple techniques of studying, and probably most of them stumbled across them more by mistake than by good management.

The quickest way between two points, say A–B, or from beginning guitarist to whatever level you want to play at, is always a straight line. However, most people follow a wavy line from bottom to top; that is, they begin on track then waver off in another direction, then get back on track again, then waver off again, and so it goes on. A lot of valuable time is wasted because it not only takes twice as long or longer to get where you want to go, but it is very frustrating and demotivating as well. This book is about practising well and for successful results.

When I first decided to become a professional guitarist, I practised eight hours a day and held a day job as well, but now I can do the same amount in half that time or less. I will share these secrets with you in this book. If you do practise eight hours every day, and have a day job, you will, of course, become a recluse and have no personal life or friends. Not a good idea.

Those who practise regularly accomplish more than those who don't. However, practising for long periods doesn't by any means guarantee success. But if we practise well, we can improve quickly. This book was written to help you improve your practice habits and have a lot more fun. Only proper planning and practising will allow you to be better than the many mediocre players there are in the world. There is a saying that goes, 'If you fail to plan, you plan to fail.'

Most beginning guitarists do not realise that everyone – no matter what style of music it is that they ultimately want to play – has to learn similar things. After all a C chord in classical is still the same C chord in rock, jazz, alternative or any other music. The way they make it sound different is in the rhythm and the guitar sound that is used.

In fifteen years of teaching guitar, questions about time management, attitudes, what to practise and the like are those most often asked. They are all interrelated and understanding how they fit together is easy. This is where this idea of the book originated. And I have noticed that all the great teachers I have studied with tend to say similar things and have similar methods. Much of their wisdom is included in this book.

I hope you really enjoy this book and that it helps you to improve your playing and gain pleasure and satisfaction from your efforts.

Kevin Downing
June, 2000

STARTING OUT

1
Prerequisites

Motivation

Before beginning the task of getting into a serious practice routine, it is a good idea to consider what your motivation is for learning to play the guitar. Is it because you want to attract members of the opposite sex? Or because your mother wants you to do it? Or because you like being centre stage?

If you play the guitar for one of these reasons, the rigours of serious study will be very difficult, but don't worry, it is easy enough to change your attitude. The great John Lennon once said in an interview that he started to play to attract the girls. His attitude towards music changed dramatically later, though. After you have studied with a good teacher for a while you will know if you are serious about the guitar or not.

Do you want to play because you can't put the instrument down? Because you are obsessed with it? Because you are a creative soul who wants to express yourself through the guitar? Because you are willing to live, sleep and eat the guitar every waking hour? If you are learning for any of these reasons then you are the type of person who could be successful.

An Open Mind

Many people realise after a short while that learning a musical instrument is nothing like they imagined. If you have any preconceived ideas about what it is going to be like, you had better forget them now. You will learn, and do many things that are new to you. However, I must stress that you will have a lot of fun doing so.

Patience

Learning music is a lifelong journey. You will never know everything there is to know about music, and you are always going to be a student. It doesn't take a lifetime to be a great guitarist though; some have done it in only a few years.

There are no shortcuts to learning how to play any musical instrument, and the guitar is no exception. If you see advertisements in the media that guarantee you can play guitar within three days or similar, ignore them, you will just be wasting your money. There is no way you can learn anything substantial in that amount of time.

We live in a world where everybody wants things instantly. After all, just about anything we want is available at the push of a button, or by producing

---

 Warning: If you think you know everything, you are in serious trouble!

---

a card. However, learning the guitar is not like that. You cannot get anyone else to practise for you; you must do it yourself. So if you are a person who seeks instant gratification, it might pay to look for something else to do with your spare time.

Music is not a race or some sort of sport; it is an art form. Certain styles of music will appeal to you, others won't. Also be prepared for change. The music business, like the fashion industry, is constantly changing. What is popular today is tomorrow's rubbish.

Discipline and patience are two virtues that most people need to work on. You too will need to develop these skills as you progress if you really want to be a succesful guitarist.

Time

Time-management is another area that needs some attention. If you are going to practise a lot and keep your social life intact, good time-management skills are essential. However, writing out a time-management plan is akin to writing out a diet. It is easy to write, but difficult to stick to.

Allow enough time for practice. Beginners normally underestimate the amount of time required. It might mean missing a favourite television programme every now and then, but it will be worth it in the long run.

The Right Equipment

Be prepared to invest some hard-earned money in equipment and books. You don't need to run out and buy everything mentioned in this book right now, but over a period of time you might well do so. You could also look at ways of borrowing some of the books and gadgets.

The guitar is completely misunderstood as an instrument. Most people will tell you that it is easy to learn. That might be true to some extent in the initial stages, but later on it is just as difficult as any other instrument. I think this myth comes from people learning to play a few party-type songs, using two or three easy chords, in a relatively short space of time.

REMEMBER
If you satisfy the prerequisites you are more likely to become a successful guitarist.

2

Talent

Talent is to a great extent about having a desire to achieve something, and then setting out to practice and learn all you can about that something – here, the guitar. You might have seen a popular poster, which reads, "Talent is 99 per cent perspiration, 1 per cent inspiration". The perspiration part relates to the fact that all talented people have to work hard to learn their craft. They learn everything they can about the particular subject they want to be talented in. Guitarists should learn as much as they can about music, and the business of music. This could take a while, depending on the amount of time that you put in, but it will be worthwhile.

The inspiration part of the poster refers to people who have the knowledge in any given area, experimenting with it and coming up with new ideas. When you put forward new ideas in music, like a new song or lick (a musical phrase or like a musical word which is part of a musical sentence), everyone will tell you that you are talented. If you read about some of the world's greatest inventions, you will find that the ideas did not just fall out of the sky into the inventor's brain. Often the inventor stumbled across them when doing something else. In other words, they were experimenting with the knowledge they had. It is a good idea to leave a little time each day to play around with the knowledge you have, to see what you can come up with. You don't need a lot of knowledge to experiment with music.

Some of the world's best songs were written this way. You might have read how a certain songwriter joined two half-completed songs together and then had a hit song. When John Lennon and Paul McCartney first began writing songs they were reported as asking guitarists for the strangest chords they knew. Then they would go and write a song around these strange chords.

A lot of solos on your favourite CDs are made up of different pieces. The musicians record five or six solos in the studio, then take a lick from each and join them all together until they have a great solo. That is what experimenting is all about. Van Halen's "Jump" solo was done this way. What can you come up with?

 REMEMBER
Talent is **99** per cent knowing your craft, **1** per cent reworking it.

3

The Importance of a Good Teacher

It amazes me that people will go out and spend two or three thousand dollars on the best equipment money can buy, and then skimp on tuition. After a short while they sell their newly-bought equipment because they are frustrated and getting nowhere. The investment in your music education is much more valuable than your guitar will ever be. Haven't you ever wondered why there are so many guitars in second-hand shops?

Teaching Yourself

Many people think that teaching themselves is the way to go, but how can you teach yourself something that you don't know anything about? Learning a musical instrument is a complicated process. You can quickly form bad habits, which are difficult to change at a later date.

There are books available which claim that they will help you teach yourself, but they are very misleading. Books are simply not interactive. How will the book tell you if you are doing something right or wrong?

Most of the best books on the market explain the main points. You still need a good teacher to explain things further. And your teacher can help you best when he or she knows what your long-term goals are.

The Benefits of Good Teaching

When you receive formal lessons from the best teachers they normally teach you how to learn. It is the "learning how to learn" part that most people miss out on. Of course, your teacher cannot teach you everything that you will eventually learn, because you will pick up little things along the way. You have most probably experienced the situation of just doodling around with your guitar and then ending up playing a song or lick that you have heard somewhere before; or of playing with a scale and coming up with a cool-sounding line. This is what most people refer to as teaching themselves, but it is really experimenting with the knowledge that they already have.

Many people think that when they learn a new lick or chord progression from a favourite CD they are teaching themselves, but really they are learning something from whoever was playing that song. When you ask a friend to show you a lick, you are learning from that friend. It is really almost impossible to teach yourself; you are always learning from someone else. Something that people find very difficult when going it alone is to motivate and encourage themselves. What guitarists really need is a good teacher and mentor who will motivate them and help them develop the work ethic needed to explore music when they are on their own.

A good teacher is also like a coach. When things are getting tough they ease you through it, and give positive feedback which helps keep you on the right track. The world's best tennis players, rugby teams and the like all have good coaches, so why shouldn't you? Superstar guitarist Brian Setzer of "The Stray Cats" said in a *Guitar Player Magazine* interview recently that he still has lessons from a jazz teacher in New York. That is probably one of the main reasons he is so good.

It saddens me when students decide to quit. What normally happens is that they stop practising, they lose their motivation, and before long they rarely play their guitar. The main reason people decide to quit lessons is to save money, but this is really false economy. It is better to have a break from the lessons, sort out the finances and then return to them. During the break, spend time perfecting and experimenting with what you have already learnt.

Finding a Teacher

Finding a good teacher can be difficult, depending on where you live. If you live in a country area, there might not be any near you. However, in a city you may have a choice of several. Always study with the best teachers; they will save you a lot of time and wasted effort. The best teachers normally charge a little more than the others, and might also have a waiting list. So get in early; if you have to wait you are wasting time.

If you don't know of any good teachers, ask at your local music store, or ask people who play themselves. The best teachers' names will keep reappearing.

Most teachers will make an appointment for an interview so they can assess what level you are at, and then discuss lesson format. If you have any questions, that is the time to ask; even have the questions written out before you arrive. If you don't feel comfortable with that teacher, try another one.

Once you have started lessons, have faith in your teacher's system. Most people have no idea what they will be required to learn. If your teacher hasn't explained why you need to know something, then ask. All teachers are different and do things in different ways, but they all have the same goal in mind. That goal is to make you the best player you can possibly be.

If you are aiming at becoming a professional, a good teacher is a must. They may have connections in the business. After I proved myself, my teacher started recommending me for gigs he couldn't do. Before long the contractors began calling me direct. By the time I was twenty-one years of age I was touring with the best performers in the world. When you move to a new city, find a good teacher no matter how advanced you are, it is the quickest way into the local scene.

Even if you go out and buy the latest Eric Clapton-model guitar, you are not going to sound like Eric Clapton; you are still going to sound like you. Your personal playing style will develop over time. It is a bit like handwriting, in that everyone has a different style. If someone blindfolded me and got all my students to play the same Eric Clapton song in turn, I would quickly be able to tell who was playing.

Some of my pupils who were originally self-taught have said to me that they wished they had started lessons right from the beginning, because they are enjoying them so much. So, why not try taking a few lessons? If you don't like them you can always quit.

If I still haven't convinced you to find a good teacher, let me ask you what you would say if you were lying on the operating table and your heart surgeon told you he was self-taught? What if the pilot of the aeroplane you were about to board told you the same thing? And by the way, good teachers teach you to read music notation, not tablature, and are more interested in the quality than the quantity of your work.

The more you learn, the more fun you will have with your instrument and your musical friends. Gaps in your knowledge and abilities really show to someone who is well-trained.

Overall your teacher should be caring and interested in you as a person and your progress, be enthusiastic, and know their craft well.

REMEMBER
A good teacher will save you a lot of frustration and time.

4

Motivation

How do people motivate themselves to practise? There are a lot of things to think about here, including your health and general well-being, your instrument, and your practice habits.

Your Health

Your health plays a big part in how you feel. If you feel good you will want to practise; if you don't feel good, practising will seem tedious.

- Try to stay fit. A gentle walk, jog, cycle, or gym workout each morning will keep you feeling good, and the more energy you have, the more motivated you will be.

- A healthy diet is also essential. Try to eat fresh fruit and vegetables each day rather than fast food. You will be amazed at the difference in the way you feel. Eating too much is a motivational killer; it makes you lethargic, so keep your food intake light. Keep your weight within its healthy range. There is truth in the saying "You are what you eat and drink".

- Drugs are a major problem if you want to be self-motivated. Stay away from them all. If you need to drink alcohol, do so in moderation. If you wake up with a hangover, you won't want to practise. Smoking causes all sorts of nastiness for your throat and lungs, so it's not a wise choice, especially if you sing.

- Good sleeping habits are essential for motivation, because if you are always tired, practising will not be stimulating. Make sure that you get a good night's sleep, but too much sleep can be just as bad as not enough, so try and regulate it to the amount that suits you.

- Your emotions can have a great effect on your motivation. If you are having problems with your life or relationships, try and get them sorted out. If you can't sort out some deep-rooted problems then seek help from a psychologist or counsellor. Try to bring humour into your life. If you can find humour in stressful situations, they become easier to deal with.

Your Guitar and Equipment

Having a good instrument, amplifier and effects, such as overdrive, chorus and delay pedals, is good for motivation. Buy the best you can afford and keep them well maintained. Always have an electronic tuner on hand. Nothing decreases motivation more than an out-of-tune guitar, so always tune up before you begin practising.

Practice Habits

Good practice habits can increase motivation. I like to warm up with things that are easy, leaving the fast and difficult things for the middle of the practice session. It is also a good idea to warm down, which is similar to warming up in that you play easier and slower things to finish, just like athletes do. If you feel any pain in your hands, arms or fingers, rest them. Pain decreases motivation.

- Regular practice for technique is essential. If you find playing scales and arpeggios every day boring, try playing them every second or third day. Try the same thing for anything else that you find dull.

- When I learn new things, I like to practise them every day for a week. After that I only play them every few days on a rotational basis. This way I don't get bored.

- Set yourself something to achieve each day. If the goal is too difficult, break it down into smaller achievable daily pieces. You will feel good when you have finished, because you will have really accomplished something.

Positive Thinking

- Think of the musical rewards that have come or will be coming your way. Playing with more accomplished guitarists, doing more prestigious gigs, going to recording sessions, having a song on national airplay – all these come to those who stick with their practice schedules.

- Look back on how much you have achieved this year. How much have you learnt? How much better are you? Tape yourself playing now, perhaps in six months, then in one year's time. Get the tape out and listen to it. Compare it to today's tape. Is there a big difference? Do this every year to track your progress. Even a one-beat-per-minute increase in tempo of a song or study you are working on is good progress, as is better control of the instrument and dynamics. There are many other ways to check your progress and your ear will tell you how much you have improved.

- Know what your long-term goal is. Read it through every day. Use positive affirmations, and say positive things about yourself. You will gradually become what you believe and have been saying about yourself. If you don't know any positive affirmations, look in bookshops or libraries for some literature on the subject. Bob Sommer's book *Psycho-Cybernetics 2000* is worth reading. If you visit the self-improvement or motivational section of your library or local bookstore, you will find many books to help you with motivation.

REMEMBER
How you practise, how you think, and how you look after yourself will increase your motivation.

5
Reading Music or Tablature

There is a lot of argument about whether guitarists should read real music or tablature.

Tablature is okay to begin with, as most people learn to talk before they can read and write, but you should wean your way off it as soon as possible. The sooner you begin to read real music notation, the more quickly you will advance as a guitar player. There is no sense in learning something that you won't need later on.

Tablature's disadvantages are that you need to hear the CD or tape to get any clue of what the music will sound like. With proper music notation you don't. A lot of music does not come with tablature (or tab for short), so you won't be able to play it. If you gave tab music to a piano player or other instrumentalist they wouldn't know what it was, and definitely would not be able to play with you. Guitarists are the only instrumentalists to use tab. Tab is playing by numbers. How many really good musicians do you know who play by numbers?

Not being able to read music is like not being able to read English. Can you imagine what that would be like? You wouldn't be able to make the grade at school, you'd be laughed at, and you'd find it very difficult to find employment. The same is true for music.

You will find people make every excuse possible to try to escape reading music. And others may say things like 'it's too hard', 'you don't need it', 'you're great already', 'it will ruin your style', and so on. Often they are people who don't read music themselves or are not very good at it.

I began just like most other guitarists: I didn't learn to read music initially. It didn't take me long to realise that if I didn't learn it I would be left behind. There were no modern guitar teachers around at the time who taught how to read music, so I enrolled with a classical guitar teacher. I have never looked back. Today, many modern guitar teachers do teach how to read music, but if you can't find one, try a classical guitar teacher, or even a piano teacher. Learning another style won't hurt you; as a matter of fact, my classical guitar training has been very beneficial to my career.

When I first began to read music, my friends gave me a hard time about it. It wasn't easy listening to them. Sometimes it was soul-destroying, but I put up with it because I knew I was on the right track. In the end everything they said just made me more determined to succeed. And today most of those people have given up the guitar, and the others who are still playing are still at the same level as they were thirty-five years ago.

Music is easier to read than English or any other language, so don't be afraid. There are only twelve notes in the musical alphabet. Some books to get you started would be *Ernie Ball Book One*, *Mel Bay's Modern Guitar Method Grade One*, or *Modern Method for Guitar* by W Leavitt. A few minutes spent reading music each day will pay big dividends later on.

Most of the best players in the world on any instrument are very good at reading music. There are some players from the old school of thought who don't read, but they are being replaced very quickly by the up-and-coming players who are very well trained.

You will often see those in orchestras and big bands reading music because their pieces are normally long and difficult to memorise. Most players in small groups such as rock bands tend to memorise theirs, because they are shorter and easier to learn. However, playing in a rock band is not an excuse for not learning to read music.

If you are planning on playing only your own compositions, or doing your own thing, you might think there is not such a pressing need to read music. However, reading music will open your mind to new and better ideas. Because they had learnt to read and write music, many of my students have written their own original songs and they are never short of new ideas. If you are unable to come up with new ideas it is because you have nothing to work with. Reading music gives you the tools to work with.

If you can't read music you are like a pilot who can't read a flight plan. How do you know what your songs are going to turn out like, or where you are really going with your music?

In today's music world, whether you want to be a professional or an amateur, you need to be a good reader *and* a good improviser. Most musicians haven't got the right mix: either they can read well but can't improvise, or they can improvise but can't read music.

If you want to be a good improviser being able to read well is a must. This is contrary to what most people think, but it is true. Ask any jazz player!

REMEMBER
The sooner you begin to read real music, the sooner you will achieve your goals.

EQUIPMENT

&

MATERIALS

6

The Practice Room

It does not really matter where you practise, as long as the area is free from noise and the other distractions normally associated with a household. A lot of my younger students use their bedrooms, and have special corners set up for the purpose. Others have a place in the garage, or even have a specially set-up room for the purpose of serious music study.

Whatever the location, it is preferable to use the same room at all times so that the equipment needed can be set up and left there. There is nothing more demotivating than having to set up and pack up after every practice session.

For Beginners

Some things for beginners to consider when setting up a practise area:

- A good chair. Choose one that is the right height or adjustable, is comfortable and will support your back.

- A footstool. If you have either short legs or a high chair, use a footstool if you sit down to practise.

- Good lighting. Always use incandescent lights rather than fluorescent ones which can cause headaches and eyestrain. Small light fittings that clip on to your music stand are also a good investment.

- Make sure the room is not too hot or cold. If it is too hot you will feel drowsy, and if it is too cold your fingers won't perform well.

- A metronome. This is essential for developing a good sense of time.

- A tape recorder. This is so you can tape yourself playing, then play the tape back and critique yourself. Just remember it won't be a studio-quality recording.

- A music stand. Choose one that can take thick, heavy books.

- An instrument stand. You can leave your guitar on this all the time. When you pass the room and see the guitar in the stand, you might want to pick it up.

Intermediate or Advanced Players

Extra things to consider for your practice room if you are an intermediate or advanced player:

- A drum machine. This is a handy piece of equipment if you want to create a lot of different grooves to play along with.

- A transcriber or slow-down machine. You can work out your favourite solos by slowing them down to different speeds. Once you have worked one out, you can practise along with the machine, working it back up to speed. Transcribers are available as stand-alone units or computer programs.

- A multitrack recorder. With this you can create your own backing tracks. You can also record yourself playing along with them. Multitrack recorders are great for song-writing as well.

- Computer programs. Programs like *Band in a Box* and other similar type recording software will help you grow. They allow you to make your own backing tracks in any style fairly easily.

- Books to practise from. Have a lot of these, especially for sight-reading. Keep them handy.

- Commercially recorded play-alongs. Those like the Jamey Aebersold series are a good investment. This series which is mainly a play-along set for jazz players has some great songs for rock players as well. Try, for instance, *How to Play and Improvise* Vol. I, *Nothin But Blues* Vol. 2, *Herbie Hancock* Vol. II, *The Magic of Miles Davis* Vol. 50. If you can't get this series from your local music store, the contact address for Jamey Aebersold Publishing is in chapter 40.

- Pictures or photos of your favourite players. These will be highly motivating hanging on your practice room walls.

REMEMBER
The right tools and a good environment will motivate you to practise.

7

The Care and Repair
of Your Instrument

When you buy equipment, whether it is a guitar, amplifier, effects or accessories, try to buy the best you can afford and take great care of it. Remember, though, that buying the Eric Clapton model Stratocaster will not necessarily make you sound like Eric Clapton. Only years of practice will do that.

Looking After Your Guitar

When it is not in use, always keep your guitar on a stand, and when travelling always have it in a good hard case, preferably a flight case. The soft cases for carrying over your shoulder do not give guitars much protection; they really only keep the rain off them. It also pays to keep a moisture absorption pad in your case so that condensation won't ruin your guitar or make the strings go rusty.

A regular polish every week will keep your instrument looking like new. The vinyl on amplifiers also looks good if you give it a regular polish.

Strings

It is a good idea to change all the strings at least every two to three months, whether you think they need it or not. If you are doing gigs, the strings will need to be changed more regularly. If you break one string, change the lot, or you will have one bright-sounding, and five dead-sounding strings. Always change the strings before you do any recording.

Always have on hand spare strings, picks, cables, fuses, batteries and anything else you might need. Strings seem to break only when the music stores are closed!

Repairs

Never try to do modifications or repairs to your guitar yourself; always leave that to a qualified repair person. I have seen many expensive instruments ruined by people trying to do their own repairs. Remember what I said earlier about self-taught people. If you really want to do your own repairs then you had better go and get some lessons from a good teacher.

It is beneficial to get your guitar checked for the action and intonation once a year. It will make it easier and more enjoyable to play. Your amplifier, cables, and effects could do with an annual check-up as well. This could save an embarrassing breakdown later. Your local music store can advise you where to get these services.

Lending Your Equipment

Do not lend your equipment to friends, unless you know they will look after it well. Nobody looks after other people's equipment as well as they do their own – just ask anyone who works in a hire centre. Many a friendship has been ruined over lent equipment coming back damaged.

REMEMBER
Proper care and maintenance of your equipment will save a lot of money and frustration.

8

Finding and Creating Practice Materials

The number of music books around is mind-boggling. I suggest you collect as many as you can. If they are general books, read through them. If they are music books, play what you can from them, or use them for sight-reading. Don't just use guitar books, but ones for other instruments as well.

I particularly like flute, saxophone and trumpet books for reading single-note lines. Piano books are great for reading chords. You will have to adjust the way you read them though, as piano players play chords with two hands. The chords are out of the guitar fingering range most of the time. The best thing to do is rearrange the chord or chords so they fit nicely within your fingering range. You have to be able to read bass clef to do this, but that isn't difficult.

I began practising from these books because in many of the gigs I was doing I had to play with the sax section, then the trombones, then the trumpets, then the piano, all in the course of one song. It was really tough because I wasn't used to playing all the different rhythm patterns that other instruments play. On some gigs where they would normally use a pianist, they would opt for a guitar instead and expect me to know some of the more prominent piano parts. After only a short time I was fluent at it. You could be too. If you are not planning on playing with varied instrumentation you might not need to do this, but it would improve your sense of rhythm and knowledge.

Other tips on finding good practice material:

• Buy the monthly guitar magazines. They have columns dedicated to certain aspects of guitar technique and repertoire. They also review the latest books and practice materials, saving you a lot of time and money.

• Visit music stores when you are in a new town. You will come across an amazing variety of books. You may even buy some books that are too advanced for you at this stage and put them away for later when you can play them comfortably.

- Share books with your musical friends, or ask for their recommendations. You can also swap books you think you will not use again, although I generally keep all mine.

- Creating your own exercises is a good idea. The students I have who do this are among the best. Do this in the areas where you have trouble playing or remembering.

- Start a lick book. When I first began, I used to file licks in a book under different categories: jazz, blues, rock, pentatonic, ii–v–1, harmonic minor, etc. Set about memorising your licks by playing them up and down the neck. After you know many good licks, piece solos together using different combinations. Write the solos out on paper if you have to.

- If you have memorised the tunes in your books, play them backwards. Yes, play them backwards! A teacher I once had would make me do this, and I realised what a good exercise it was. This works best for single-line playing.

- If the tunes seem easy, speed them up or play them in cut time (i.e. two instead of four beats to the bar). This will save you a lot of money in practice materials.

REMEMBER
Informed people – whether they are guitarists or not – normally have a large collection of books to refer to.

PRACTICE – GENERAL TIPS

9
The Six Things you Need to Practise

After you have mastered the basics – open chords, bar chords and simple single-note reading – the six most important practice areas are technique, repertoire, sight-reading, ear training, theory, and general knowledge.

Technique

Technique is the result of hand–brain coordination and fingerboard knowledge. It can only be gained by the regular practice of scales, arpeggios, chords and melodic patterns played in all possible positions over the neck. Having good technique will enable you to play any song in any key or style. People who say they don't care about good technique are only fooling themselves. You will never be a good player without it.

Repertoire

Repertoire is the learning and memorising of many tunes in your chosen area of study. This includes chord progressions as well as any solos. Get transcriptions of the songs you want to learn, or write them out yourself, then learn them slowly. Once you have the song up to performance speed, play along with it. Every technique you have learnt previously will be used in these songs, so good technique development is essential.

Sight-reading

Sight-reading is the art of being able to play a sheet of music immediately, with no mistakes, the first time. Sounds incredible? It can be achieved through daily sight-reading practice. Being a good sight-reader really does give you the edge over other guitarists.

Ear-Training

Nobody is born with a musical ear; training your ear is the only way you can develop one. The benefits of ear training are immense. You will be able to hear chord progressions and solos, and play them immediately by ear.

Theory

The study of music theory is also very helpful. It enables you to understand how chords are built, how to compose music and arrange it, how to transpose, and how to write music out for your band.

General Knowledge

General knowledge is about knowing the history of the music you are interested in, from its very beginnings to the present day. Reading biographies of the performers is also interesting. Knowing about the leading artists and having a good working knowledge of their different styles will enhance your guitar playing.

REMEMBER
Technique, repertoire, sight-reading, ear-training, theory and general knowledge are the six things you need to practise.

10

Technique

More is Better

You should devote some time each day to improving your technique. Techniques that you could study include fingerstyle, chord-melody, comping, soloing, scales, and arpeggios. There are many others.

Because there are hundreds of different techniques, you might not need to learn them all. For example, if you are a rock guitarist you might not want to learn chord-melody style, which is mainly a jazz technique. If you are a classical guitarist you might leave out soloing. However, it is good to learn as many as you possibly can.

When it comes time to play a song, there might be anything from two to ten different techniques within it. Even if there is only one technique in that song you don't know, it will be a constant struggle to play it effortlessly.

The people who argue against having good technique are normally the people who haven't got any themselves, and are too lazy to practise. If you have great technique already, try playing a wider range of music and learning new techniques you haven't tried. It will broaden your knowledge and approach to the music you play.

Some good books to get you going are *Modern Method for Guitar* by W. Leavitt, and for fingerstyle, *Solo Guitar Playing* by F. Noad, or *Classic Guitar Technique* by Aaron Shearer. These books do not have every technique you will need to know, but are a good starting point. The more techniques you know, the better you are going to be and the more gigs and jam sessions you will enjoy later on.

Twelve Keys

Try to learn everything you can in twelve keys. Chord progressions and licks are especially important. Most guitarists are not very good at playing in twelve keys, but there is a good reason why you should practise this skill. If you play with different instrumentalists this is what will happen: pianists like to play in the keys of C, F and G, horn players tend to play in F, Bb, Eb and Ab and if you are going to play in a stage show like 'Phantom of the Opera', or 'Jesus Christ Superstar', you can expect any of the twelve keys. How prepared would you be if someone asked you to play with a sax player or do a stage show?

Sometimes when you hear a song it sounds easy, and when you see professionals playing, it looks easy too. Then when you come to play the song, you find it is not – it is much faster than you imagined, and in other ways so much more difficult to play than you thought it would be. This is because the professionals have put thousands of hours or even lifetimes into practising their technique. If you want to play the same songs as the pros, you too will have to put in a lot of time practising technique.

Pace and Precision

Always begin learning any new technique very slowly, making sure your fingering and pick or finger attack is correct. In other words, that you are playing it the same way slowly as you are going to play it fast. Only then can you work it up to speed with the metronome.

Try to get used to using hard picks (1mm or more); they are better for playing faster lines because they are less flexible.

Once you have a good technique for the music you want to play, you can forget the fingerings and pick directions and all other technique-related things, and just concentrate on the music. Playing with great feeling only comes after technique is so well rehearsed you don't have to think about it.

There will be times when you think you are practising like crazy and not getting any better. Don't worry! Some things take a bit of time to get into our fingers and brains. If you persevere, the techniques will eventually come. Sometimes you may find you have acquired a particular technigue you have been practising, without being aware of it.

REMEMBER
You need good technique to be a great guitarist. Work on your techniques each day and you will rise above the many mediocre players.

11

Learning a Repertoire

First of all decide on the style of music you want to play. Then make a list of at least fifty to seventy of the most-played songs of that style. Search for the CDs or tapes and the music or transcriptions of these songs. Your teacher might be able to help out here. If the music is unavailable, you might have to transcribe the music yourself or get a friend to do it.

After you have gathered some music and tapes, set about learning the songs, starting with the easiest ones. Try for one tune a week, although realise some of the more difficult ones could take longer. After a year you will have a reasonable repertoire.

If you are a rock, blues or country player, make sure you learn the rhythm and lead parts. Jazz players should learn the head, comping and a few solos. No matter what style you are learning, pay close attention to the little nuances such as time, groove, phrasing, chord progressions and form of the tune. You will learn a lot from this.

After you have learnt the song, it is a good idea to play along with the CD or tape. This will give you the feel of playing the song in a band situation. The more you play along with your favourite bands, the more quickly you will progress. Try to copy everything your favourite players are doing. Before long you will be inventing your own ways of doing things.

It is a good idea to get the feel of one style before moving on to another. The best guitarists are good at more than one style, in fact they are good at many.

REMEMBER
If you know how to play more than one style well, you will be well on your way to being a very good guitarist.

12

Improving Your Sight-Reading

There are two levels of music reading: reading and sight-reading. If you have to work the music out note by note, you can read it, but this is too slow. Sight-reading means you can play whatever is put in front of you immediately. This is the level to aspire to. It means that you will be able to learn new tunes quickly. Most other instrumentalists can do it, so why not guitarists?

Sight-reading can be improved simply by reading as much music as you can. They don't need to be guitar books. I use violin, flute, sax and trumpet books, as well as rhythm-study books for guitar. Some good ones are: *Melodic Rhythms for Guitar* by William Leavitt, *Reading Contemporary Guitar Rhythms* by M. T. Szymczak, *Jazz Conception* by Jim Snidero and *Reading Key Jazz Rhythms* by Fred Lipsius.

If you are just starting out, *Ernie Ball Phase One* and *Phase Two*, the *Mel Bay Book One*, or *Howard Roberts Guitar Manual Sight-Reading* would be very useful.

Begin a piece slowly, and don't stop for mistakes. If you keep getting lost, then slow down. Speed will come later. Once you have finished a piece, go on to the next one immediately. The idea is to play through a lot of music rather than perfect it. Perfection will come later. As your ability to read improves, you can work the metronome speed up slowly, or increase the difficulty level.

A good idea that I learned many years ago is to have a pile of books to play out of each day. Keep them open ready for playing. Play a couple of pages from the top one, then place it at the bottom of the pile. Then take the next one, play a couple of pages, and put it at the bottom of the pile, and so on. This way you will not play the same thing every day. You are sight-reading and cannot memorise the music. Change the books every few months.

If you have trouble playing and reading rhythms at the same time, just play everything as quarter-notes to get your fingers around it. Once you can do that, work out the rhythm. It is a good idea to tap the rhythm out before playing it on your guitar. Always remember that music notation tells you two things: the note you have to play, and the length of time that note must last for. It takes time to master this, so take it easy.

Most guitar books these days come with normal music notation as well as tab. It is a good idea to cover the tab so it doesn't distract you. You can do this by cutting thin strips of plain paper – just wide enough to cover the tab

– and glueing them over the tab line in your book. The tablature also makes you very tired when practising because it is always in your peripheral vision. Tiring yourself unnecessarily when practising is something you should avoid.

If you haven't got the money to invest in a lot of music books, borrow some from your friends, or try your local library.

REMEMBER
The better you can sight-read, the more quickly you learn. Before long the gigs will start coming your way.

13

Ear-Training

Have you ever wondered how people can listen to the radio or a CD and instantly play what they are hearing? Well, if you practise ear-training a little each day, you too will soon be able to do it.

Our ear has to be trained like any other of our sense organs. If your eyes can see the colour red, why shouldn't your ears be able to hear a Bb? Many people have some form of ear perception already. If you can tell the speed of your car by the sound of its engine, or what kind of car is passing, by the sound it makes, that is a form of ear perception. In other words you have trained your ear over a period of time to hear those things.

There are many ear-training courses available from music retailers. The *Jamey Aebersold Jazz Ear Training Course* would be a good place to begin. You don't need to be a jazz player to do this course; it is for anyone.

Pitch

There are two types of ear perception. One is called relative pitch, the other is perfect pitch. Relative pitch is judging the musical relationship between two notes or chords when you know what the first one is. Perfect pitch is when you hear a note or chord and can tell exactly what it is, with no reference to any other note.

Relative pitch is used most in music performance, and should be practised daily. Perfect pitch courses are now available, but are more advanced. I suggest you begin with a good relative pitch course.

Intervals

If you are not using an ear-training course, you can begin by listening to the twelve intervals in music. What you do is relate a song you already know to the required interval, which then makes it easier to remember. If the note C is played then F, slowly you will begin to hear the tune 'Love Me Tender' by Elvis Presley. The first two notes of that tune are C to F in the key of C major. This is called a perfect fourth interval. If you know your theory, performing perfect fourths in any key will be easy.

Hearing them is easy as well, because all intervals sound the same in every key, whether they are played in a high or low register. They also sound the same on every instrument. After you know what the intervals sound like, get some of your non-guitar friends to play some for you on their instruments. You will quickly get used to being able to tell the intervals on other instruments.

Major second	C followed by D	'Polly Wolly Doodle'
Major third	C followed by E	'Oh When the Saints'
Perfect fifth	C followed by G	'Twinkle Twinkle Little Star'
Major sixth	C followed by A	'My Bonnie'
Major seventh	C followed by B	'Cast your Fate to the Wind' (also sounds dissonant and horrible)
Perfect octave	C followed by C (an octave higher)	'Somewhere Over the Rainbow'
Minor second	C followed by Db	'I Remember You'
Minor third	C followed by Eb	'Georgia On My Mind'
Minor seventh	C followed by Bb	'Star Trek Theme'
Augmented fourth	C followed by F#	'Maria' (from *West Side Story*)
Augmented fifth	C followed by G#	'The Entertainer'

The twelve intervals with their related songs are shown below.

If you don't know any of the songs mentioned above, don't worry. Many more songs begin with the same intervals. Try to find some with which you are familiar. For example, if you are a rock guitarist, Jimi Hendrix's song 'Purple Haze' begins with a perfect octave.

Once you have a good grasp of the ascending intervals, work on hearing them descending. It is a little more difficult to find songs with descending intervals, but if you are alert you will find some. You could also just sing and play ascending intervals backwards.

When you are practising the intervals on your instrument, play them slowly and just listen. Once you have the sound in your ear, sing them as well – I teach my students to sing the letter names of the notes or just use la la – it helps to recognise them even quicker. Your favourite lead lines or licks are just a succession of intervals and it won't be very long before you will be able to work them all out.

Chords

You can recognise chords by their particular sound. Here are some to get

Major chords	sunny day or happy sound
Minor chords	cloudy day or sad sound
Dominant chords	unstable (want to resolve to their relative major chord)
Diminished chords	spooky sounding (horror movies and cartoons) connecting chord

When practising chords try to hear the sunny day or happy quality in the major sound, and the sad sound in the minor. Singing the arpeggio of the chord will help you to internalise the sound as well; for example, sing the notes C, E, G, C, individually for the major triad.

Later on, when transcribing the chords of your favourite songs you will be able to hear the quality of the chords being played, as well as the distance that they move, by identifying the intervals.

Playing along with the radio or CD and transcribing music is a form of ear-training which you should try as soon as possible. If you have someone else who can practise with you, playing ear-training games is quite fun. This is one that I like. One of you plays a note and the other one plays the same note on his or her instrument. If you don't get it right the first time, you have another try, then another and so on until you get it right. Then swap positions. The person who made the fewest attempts wins. You can also do this with chords and scales.

I once heard a story about the legendary guitarist Larry Carlton. Apparently he used to carry a Kratt Chromatic Pitch Pipe with him everywhere he went. When he heard a sound, he would play what he thought it was on his pitch pipe. If he was wrong, he would name the interval and then play the correct note. Why not try this.

Our ears are sensitive pieces of equipment. Make sure you look after them. Don't have your headphones or amplifiers too loud. If you attend loud concerts, invest in a good set of earplugs and carry them with you. If you work in a noisy environment, always wear hearing protection.

REMEMBER
A well-trained ear is the most important asset a musician can have.

43

14
Theory

A knowledge of theory will give you the ability to understand what is going on within the music you are playing, and to know the rules that everyone else works by.

A good guitarist must know things like key signatures, scales, chord scales and construction, chord substitution, time signatures, melody, melody harmonisation, intervals, transposition, triads, composition and a whole host of other things too numerous to mention here.

Lots of people never learn theory because the guitar is an instrument where most things are easily transposed up or down the neck to the various keys. Don't be fooled. You still need to study theory.

A good introductory course is *Master Your Theory* by Dulcie Holland. This is a series of seven books. You could leave out the classical theory bits if you are concentrating on modern music. Advanced students could try *The Jazz Language* by Dan Haerle. This book is not just for jazz players but anyone who improvises up to advanced levels. There are other books that are just as good, but these are the ones I use for my students.

Learning as much about theory as you can really does increase your ability to do many things:

- Transcribing – because you will know what to listen for.
- Composing – you will know what the pros do.
- Transposing – this will be second nature after a while.
- Arranging – learning to write music for instruments other than your own. This also includes writing for small to large ensembles.
- How other instruments work – so you can play them if you wish to.

There are very few days when a musician doesn't draw on his or her theory training.

REMEMBER
It pays to know the rules before you break them.

15

General Knowledge

When I first began to play the guitar I didn't read many books. I was too interested in playing. Now I read a lot. The books that are available today make the job of playing a lot easier and more interesting. If you take just fifteen minutes a day to read books, you will become a much more knowledgeable guitarist.

Magazines

Any of the monthly guitar magazines are worth reading. They are all excellent. They usually have a column dedicated to reviewing the new books and videos available for guitarists.

Books

Some of the books I recommend you have are:

For Guitar Players Only, by Tommy Tedesco
Gibson Electrics, by A.R. Duchossoir
Improve Exam Results in 30 Days, by Harry Lorayne
Modern Recording Techniques, by Huber & Runstein
The Oxford Companion to Music
The Grove Dictionary of Music
The Grove Dictionary of Jazz
The New Grove Gospel, Blues and Jazz, by Oliver, Harrison & Bolcom
The Guitar Handbook, by Ralph Denyer
The Fender Stratocaster, by A.R. Duchossoir

This list is not exhaustive; it is only to get you started or to whet your appetite for more information. Check your local library for more titles. Second-hand shops are also great places to pick up cheaply priced as well as hard-to-find books.

It is a good idea to read the biographies or autobiographies of your favourite players. Also check out some famous people who are not guitar players to see what they did to get to where they are. It makes an interesting study.

The evolution of the guitar is also a fascinating study. Stringed instruments were among the first instruments to be invented. See if you can find any books on the history of the guitar.

Videos

There seem to be a lot of videos on the market today which not only deal with the how-to-play aspect of guitar, but also the history and life stories of famous artists. They are also worth checking out.

REMEMBER
Just fifteen minutes' reading each day will make you a much more knowledgeable musician.

PRACTICE – MORE
ADVANCED TIPS

16
Lists of Goals and the Practice Log

Your Long-term Goal

It is very important that you know what you want to achieve. What level do you want to get to – amateur, semi-professional or professional? An amateur is someone who plays for the pure enjoyment of it without receiving any payment. A semi-professional is someone who holds a day job, but receives additional payment for his or her musical services. These people normally play in bands or are soloists for weddings, parties, clubs, etc. The majority of guitarists are in this category. A professional guitarist is someone who lives solely on the money they receive from playing guitar.

Your goal could be that you want to play with a local band, make your own CD, or become a session player. These are realistic goals which most people can achieve. A goal to be the best guitarist in the world, or to become the next superstar is unrealistic and would probably not be achievable.

Now you should work out the length of time you would like it to take to reach that goal. Be realistic here; if you want to be a professional it could take ten years. Your teacher or an experienced friend can help you calculate this. Now write this goal on a piece of paper and hang it on the wall in your practice room.

Annual Goal

Over the page is a list of goals. Now that you know your long-term goal, it is not difficult to work out an annual goal, which you should write on your wall chart. A good goal for your first year might be to play half of *Modern Method for Guitar* by W. Leavitt, learn fifty songs, play through a lead guitar book, play through a sight-reading book, and have done a few performances.

Monthly Goals

Next, work out your monthly and weekly objectives by dividing all your technique studies, repertoire, and reading studies. Write these on the chart.

Memo

My Long-term Goal
To be a semi-professional guitarist in three years
(this assumes you know the basics or are near an intermediate level).

Annual Goal (over three years)
✓ To play Modern Method for Guitar (Books 1 and 2).
✓ Play the Lead Rock Method (Books 1 and 2) and know at least 150 songs.
✓ Learn theory, ear-training, some listening and reading.

Monthly Goal
✓ Play and learn seven pages from Modern Method for Guitar (Books 1 and 2).
✓ Play and learn four pages from Lead Rock Method (Books 1 and 2).
✓ Learn four songs.
✓ Theory, ear-training, listening and reading — seven hours.

Weekly Goal
✓ Play and learn two pages from Modern Method for Guitar (Books 1 and 2).
✓ Play and learn one page from Lead Rock Method (Books 1 and 2).
✓ Learn one song.
✓ Theory, ear-training, listening and reading — 15 minutes on alternative days.

The Practice Logs — Monthly and Weekly (See pp. 50 and 51)

Now write in what you are going to practise for the month under the monthly tasks column on your Practice Log, and fill in the daily column as you complete the practice. The daily column would include page numbers or some other record of what you had practised.

Practice Log

Weekly Goal:_____

Monday	
Tuesday	
Wednesday	
Thursday	
Friday	
Saturday	
Sunday	

Note: You can create a similar Log showing the twelve months of the year.

Practice Log

Annual Goal

96 Pages Modern Method for Guitar
Lead Rock Method Book 1
52 songs – theory, ear-training, listening & reading

Monthly Objective

Seven pages Modern Method for Guitar
Four pages Lead Rock Method. Four songs
Theory, ear-training, listening & reading (7 hrs)

Monthly Tasks

Monthly Tasks	1	2	3	4	5	6	7	8	9	10	11	12	13	14	15	16	17	18	19	20	21	22	23	24	25	26	27	28	29	30	31
Modern Method Review	4/10	11/15	15/19	4/10	11/15	15/19	4/10	11/16	17/4	5/11	12/19	4/11	12/19	4/10	11/16	17/5	6/11	12/19	4/11	12/19	6/11	12/18	19/6	7/12	13/19	4/16	11/16	17/5	6/11	12/18	
Lead Rock Review	5/7	8/10	5/7	8/10	5/7	8/10	11/13	8/10	11/13	14/16	11/13	14/16	14/16	17/18	17/20	19/18	17/20	19/18	17/20	19/20	21/22	23/24	21/22	23/24	21/11	23/24					
New Work	✓	✓	✓	✓	✓	✓	✓	✓	✓	✓	✓	✓	✓	✓	✓	✓	✓	✓	✓	✓	✓	✓	✓	✓							
Songs: Layla	✓	✓	✓	✓	✓	✓	✓	✓	✓	✓	✓													✓							
Smoke on the Water								✓	✓	✓	✓	✓	✓	✓	✓	✓	✓	✓													
Stairway to Heaven													✓	✓	✓	✓	✓	✓	✓	✓	✓	✓	✓	✓					✓		
Johnny B Good																					✓	✓	✓	✓			✓		✓		
Theory	✓				✓											✓			✓			✓									
Ear-training		✓							✓					✓			✓														
Listening						✓					✓								✓					✓							
Reading				✓				✓				✓				✓				✓					✓						
Change Strings																															
Day of the Month	1	2	3	4	5	6	7	8	9	10	11	12	13	14	15	16	17	18	19	20	21	22	23	24	25	26	27	28	29	30	31

Page 51 shows what your practise log would look like when it is filled out. There is also a weekly practice log, which some people will prefer. Whichever one is for you, draw a chart up for yourself, or write your own version. The important thing is that you have a record and know what you are doing each day.

Most of my students keep their practice logs in a notebook. You can record other things in the notebook as well, such as service schedules for your equipment.

If after a month you haven't achieved what you set out to do, don't worry. Sometimes it takes a while to settle in. See how you are going after two months. If you are still not achieving, maybe you have set yourself too much to do, or you need more time to practise.

If you have a lot of things to practise and can't fit them all into one day, do some things every second or third day.

Your goals need not be rigid. If you feel they aren't working, change them.

REMEMBER
Write down your goals and read them every day.

17

How Much Practice?

The amount of practice you need to do will depend on your long-term goal. Your rate of success will depend on how much time you have available, and how much of that you put into practising.

How Long?

Here are a few suggestions to think about.

- If you are new to the guitar you need to spend a minimum of thirty minutes per day practising. If you have a good knowledge of another instrument, the time required would still need to be the same, but you will advance a little more quickly, because you probably already read music and know some theory.

- Amateur guitarists or advanced beginners should be able to advance at a good rate on one hour's practice per day.

- If you want to be a semi-professional – that is someone who has a day job but plays gigs on the weekends for money – two hours' practice a day would suffice.

- If you want to be a professional you should be practising four to six hours per day. Some of that time should be devoted to other music-related subjects such as ear-training and theory. You could put in less time but it will take longer to achieve your goals. Do more and you will get there more quickly.

How Often?

Practising seven days a week is the only way to advance quickly. Six days is the minimum amount. If you cannot practise for six days a week, improvements in your playing ability will be very slow. If you can only practise three or four days a week, you will hardly see any improvement in your playing ability at all. One or two practice days a week means you are wasting your time and you should decide whether guitar is really what you want to do.

When practising, short sessions are more beneficial than long ones. If you are practising three hours per day, then three one-hour sessions will be more productive than one three-hour session. If you are doing one hour per day, cut it into two half-hour sessions.

Everybody is different and you must find something that works for you. If your mind starts to wander, it is time to have a break. Take five or ten minutes rest, then begin again. Some people do a little in the morning, some in the afternoon, and some at night. Find the pattern that works for you.

When beginning your practice session it is a good idea to have a clock or watch nearby so you don't go overtime on any one subject. Put the answerphone on and tell other people in your house that you are not to be disturbed. Make sure you feel comfortable before beginning: loosen tight clothing, don't eat too much, and go to the bathroom first.

If you experience pain while practising, stop immediately and give your hands a rest. Come back to it in a few minutes. If you experience pain that does not go away you should stop for a few days or even a week. If the pain persists, see a doctor. During this downtime you could do some composition, theory study, or some mind practice (see page 22).

REMEMBER
If you miss one day's practice, you will notice.
If you miss two days' practice, your friends will notice.
If you miss three days' practice, everybody notices.

18
Keep Within Your Limits

One thing you might already know is that you will have good and bad days when practising. The good days are no problem and you should pat yourself on the back for doing a great job of the practice session. The bad days can be a source of real frustration and are the reason a lot of players give up. Here are a few guidelines to help you.

- Keep things slow. If you are having trouble doing anything, slow it down. You know the phrase "speed kills"? Going too fast too quickly will kill your progress. If there are any flaws (missed notes, buzzes, losing time, etc.) in your playing, you are going too fast. Slow down until there are no flaws.

- Use a metronome. This is important because when you begin playing guitar it is common to want to go fast. If you haven't got a metronome, the tempos you select to play your pieces each day will be erratic, and will compound the bad-day effect. Try to keep all beginner exercises in the 50–60 beats per minute range. This is the best way of working on your speed. Work out a comfortable tempo for the song or study you are working on, then write it down at the top of the music. At a comfortable tempo you should be able to play the piece reasonably well without mistakes. Only work the speed up when you are really used to the last tempo. When you can play a piece through with no mistakes at least three times, you are ready to move up. Make sure to write the new tempo at the top of the page.

- Choose appropriate material. Quite often beginners try to play things that are way above their ability, such as a Jimi Hendrix solo when they can't play a simple melody like 'Love Me Tender'. If you are doing this, you are wasting your practice time. Ask your teacher or an experienced friend whether what you are trying to achieve is within your limits. Don't worry, you will be able to play the difficult piece later, when you are more experienced. If you do go beyond your limits, be prepared for some big disappointments.

- Avoid tiredness. Tiredness contributes to the bad-day effect and should be avoided. The best time to practise – although it isn't always possible – is early in the morning when you are fully alert.

- Know your physical limits. Do not strain the muscles in your arms, hands and fingers. The only thing you should be stretching is your creative limit.

REMEMBER
Keep within your physical limits, but try to stretch your creative limits.

19

Listening

One thing that can be a problem for people who are beginning to play the guitar is their failure to listen to good guitar playing. You can't learn if you don't listen to a lot of guitar music. I have come across people in my seminars who are beginning the guitar but can't name a single guitar player because they have never consciously listened to one.

Listening to background music is not quality listening. Investing in a good set of headphones and a stereo is a good start. Listening attentively is best done if you put on your headset, close your eyes and then listen. You can hear so much more with your eyes shut.

What is best to listen to? Listen to your favourite players first, then find out who they listen to. You can discover this by reading interviews in the monthly guitar magazines. When I began, I compiled a list of all the guitarists I could think of, going right back to the 1930s. Then I set about procuring some of the recordings. I listened extensively to them and learnt every song on the albums.

It is a good idea to listen to a lot of different types and styles of music. You will be amazed at how much you will learn by doing this. You can do this by visiting your local library, borrowing from friends, changing radio stations frequently and buying a new album regularly.

In my collection I have music dating back centuries, and right up to the many styles available today. I not only listen to learn new things, but also for enjoyment, relaxation and inspiration; and to satisfy my changing moods.

Getting out and listening to live music is a must. Support your local musicians by going to their gigs and they will reciprocate by coming along to yours. Don't forget that stage shows also have bands, musicians and other types of entertainers.

A lot of musicians never listen to themselves when they are practising or performing. If you are not listening to the sound reproduction of your performance, you are more than likely going to sound bad. Recording yourself every now and then is a good idea. Play the recording back. What do you think? Don't take the recording quality into account, but you can tell if you are making mistakes, need a better overdrive sound or any other of a thousand things. Don't be overly critical of yourself at this stage though – unless you are a professional.

Most of the world's best performers record their concerts every night, then evaluate them afterwards. They normally video the show once a week as well. That is why they are world-class; they are constantly striving to improve their performance.

When you have a song ready for performance, ask yourself these questions:

- Does it sound better on the front, middle or back pickup?
- Am I using too much overdrive? (a common problem)
- Am I using too many effects?
- Should I play with fingers or a pick?
- Should I slide some notes or hammer on?
- Is this voicing (i.e. chord chosen) a good one for the song or should I change it?
- Does the solo fit the song or not?
- Could this song sound better played with an acoustic guitar?

There are many more.

REMEMBER
Listen, listen and listen.

20
How to Make Practising Fun

It is important to learn how to balance the fun parts of practising with the parts that can quickly get boring.

Scales and Arpeggios

- One way is to practise the boring things such as scales and arpeggios for very short periods of time, say, five minutes, but do them two or three times a day.

- Another way to practise scales and arpeggios is to make your own backing tracks by playing the chords onto a cassette tape or CD. You can record them through the cycle of fourths or play them chromatically up and down the fingerboard. Playing along with the tracks will automatically make practising more fun. Playing one chord per bar will allow you to play up and down any major, minor or eight-note scale using quavers or eighth notes. If you have a scale with fewer than eight notes, adjust the rhythm to suit.

- Scales, arpeggios and licks are great things to practise while watching television. The next time your favourite movie or sport is on try it; the television helps to prevent it becoming boring. If other people are watching with you, don't play loudly; even better, use an unplugged electric guitar.

Use Your Equipment

- Making use of your recording gear, band-in-a-box (a computer programme on which you can make your own backing tracks), rhythm machines or drum machines is one of the best ways to have fun and improve very quickly as well. It is worth spending a few minutes each day learning how to work them.

- If you own an electric guitar and some effect pedals, use some of the effects on the songs or exercises that you are practising. The key here is to experiment to see what you can come up with that sounds good. Just remember that effects don't hide bad guitar playing! You should be able to play the exercises or songs well before employing the effects.

- If you need to practise a solo for your band or some other performance, record the backing chords onto tape or use a rhythm machine and then play or work out some ideas for the song. When you go to the next rehearsal or performance you should be able to play the solo really well.

This is a good method to use when learning licks (licks are like musical words). If you have a few blues licks, record a blues progression and play them through. If you have some rock licks, record some of your favourite rock progressions and do the same.

When you are playing a duet piece, always record the other part, then play along with the recording so you will know what the piece sounds like in performance. It will save you some rehearsal time as well.

Variety

- One thing that makes practising boring is doing the same things day after day for long periods of time. Try to vary everything that you do. Keep many different things on your music stand to practise, and don't allow yourself too much time on any one of them – say, no longer than fifteen minutes.

- When you know a piece of music in one area of your guitar, play it in another, or change the octave up or down. This is fun, and challenging as well.

- Ask some of your musical friends how they make practising fun; maybe they may have some new ideas for you.

- Build up a library of backing tracks to your favourite songs so you can play along with them whenever you want to. Playing along with CDs is another fun way of practising. This way, it is like playing in the same band as your heroes. Try to add little licks between the vocal lines if you can. When it comes to the solo, play exactly what is on the CD. You can also make up your own solo. To do this you will need to shut out the recorded solo by just making out it is not there. This takes time, but you will get used to it. I used to spend a lot of time doing this when I first began and I still do it now. Many of the world's greatest players do it too.

Rewards

Rewarding yourself with something small (such as playing some favourite songs, having a favourite food or drink or watching a TV programme) after a successful practice session is a good idea. After you have achieved your annual or long-term goal a larger reward is in order – perhaps a trip overseas or a new guitar!

REMEMBER
Always be on the lookout for more ways to make practising fun.

21
Rhythm Guitar

Rhythm guitar seems to be a lost art at the moment. In general, everyone wants to be the next guitar-slinging hero. A big word of caution here; listen to the rhythm playing on your guitar hero's albums. You will be surprised at how good they are at it. If you intend to play in a band or with your friends, you will be required to play some sort of rhythm guitar style about 95 per cent of the time, and solos only about five per cent of the time.

One reason people overlook rhythm guitar playing is that the lead player or soloist seems to get most of the limelight. Most people seem to want to be a star! Another reason is that good rhythm guitar is not that easy to play. Soloing only uses one finger most of the time. Chords or triads in rhythm guitar have to be played with more than one finger at a time, making it more difficult to get around the fretboard. The strumming hand also has a difficult time, especially when the music is at a quick tempo and in some of the Latin styles.

When I first began to do gigs I found out very quickly that it was my backup guitar playing that people wanted, even though I could play solos like the best of them. Even today on some gigs I might only get one or two solos.

When learning the art of rhythm guitar it really pays to learn as many styles as you can. One that is a favourite amongst the many people I have worked with over the years is funk. If you are a player who can play funky picking lines and chords well, you will be in great demand.

There are many good books available on the subject of rhythm guitar and more are constantly coming onto the market. Purchase as many as you can, and take the time to learn them. There are rhythm licks, just as there are solo licks. You need to learn the ones most frequently used and have them memorised in as many keys as possible. When practising your chord and triad studies, always try for a smooth sound. In other words, all the strings should sound at the same volume. It isn't easy, but it's well worth the effort.

A lot of rhythm guitar is based on triads, so learning the triad shapes all over the neck is advisable. They are all covered in the *Modern Method for Guitar* books by W. Leavitt. Another good book is *Guitar Comping* by Barry Galbraith.

 REMEMBER
Strive to be good at both rhythm and lead styles.

22

Using Your Time More Efficiently

Do you wake up in the morning then lie in bed and stare at the ceiling for thirty minutes? Why not get out of bed and practise? You will have an extra thirty minutes practice every day. Do you sleep too much? Most people can get by easily with less sleep. Begin by setting your alarm clock fifteen minutes earlier each week for two weeks, then the same again for another two weeks. Suddenly you have an extra half an hour to practise, and I bet you won't feel much different.

I was talking to the famous guitarist Frank Gambale a few years ago. He told me that when he first arrived in L.A. he had to practise a lot because he wanted to be very good in a short space of time. To achieve this he hardly ever slept. He gradually acclimatised his body to function without much sleep so he could practise more. He never really missed the sleep because his mind was so focused on the guitar. After a while the rest of his flatmates began to do the same thing. It certainly worked, because after only three years or so he had become one of the best guitarists in the world!

You do not need to go to this extreme, but there are many other ways to increase your practice time, such as cutting down your television viewing, or recording the programmes you want to watch and fast-forwarding through the advertisements. Using the telephone instead of going somewhere in person will save a lot of time, especially if you live in a large city. If you need to go somewhere in the car, try to do several jobs in one trip.

Here are some more tips on making the best use of your practice time:

• Practise first thing in the morning if you can; this is when your mind is wide awake. If you practise late at night your mind is normally tired, so you won't practise well and it will generally take longer. Some people like to split their practice between morning and night. Then there are people who are just not morning people and who only practise at night. Whatever works for you, do that. Don't change something if it works for you.

• On your days off or your holidays, practise first thing in the morning, before your friends begin to call. If you spend the day at the beach, or doing a lot of physical things, it is highly likely you will not feel like practising when you get home.

- If you are a student, see if you can double your practice over the holiday period. This will result in approximately three months' extra practice per year.

- Tell the people who live with you that you don't want to be disturbed while practising. Ask them to take phone messages for you, then get back to the callers after you have finished. Most non-musicians think that playing music is not a serious thing to do, so you will have to educate them.

- Each day when you sit down to practise, have something small that you want to achieve. Maybe you can learn a favourite lick really well, play a rhythm figure that you find difficult, or something else you can achieve within the timeframe of your practice session. If for some reason you don't achieve your goal, try to do so the next day.

- Everything that you practice should also relate to your long-term goal. Be flexible; if something gets boring, move on to the next thing immediately. You can always come back to it later.

REMEMBER
If you use your time efficiently, you will do a lot more practice.

23

Improving Your Musical Memory

A lot of people ask how they can improve their memory. Believe me you don't have to be a whizz-kid to do this; it is quite easy.

There are times when a performer needs to have a major part of the performing repertoire memorised. It doesn't look right to be reading music in a rock band or small ensemble. However, if you play in a big band or orchestra, reading music is the accepted practice.

Rock and pop tunes are normally fairly easy to remember. They only last a few minutes and are normally of the verse, verse, chorus, verse, chorus, or A A B A B variety. Remembering the form of a song is one way of memorising it.

If you are a jazz player the repertoire will be a bit more difficult. There is an excellent book available called *How to Learn Tunes* by David Baker. I recommend it to all guitar players.

A lot of songs sound the same as others. You have probably noticed this already. These songs are called "contrafacts", which is the term used to describe the substitution of one set of vocals for another without changing the music too much. You can hear this a lot in the blues, rock, country and jazz genre.

The songs 'Rock Around the Clock', 'See You Later Alligator', 'Guitar Boogie', 'Good Golly Miss Molly', 'Mean Woman Blues', 'Johnny B Goode' and 'Roll Over Beethoven', all use the twelve-bar blues chord progression. If you know how the blues progression and its variations work, you will automatically have many songs memorised.

A lot of pop-rock type tunes use chord progressions such as blues progressions or I–IV–V, I–V, I–VI–IV–V. Thinking in this fashion makes it easy to learn simple pop songs. Learning the Roman numeral system for chords means you can transpose any memorised song to any other key, which is also a worthwhile thing to know. In the key of C major, the Roman numerals would be C-1, Dmi-II, Emi-III, F-IV, G7-V, Ami-VI, Bmi7b5-VII.

Repetition is the only way to install things in your long-term memory, so it is a good idea to play the songs you want to memorise each day. To make this repetition exciting, play along with a recording.

There is no doubt that if you are playing for a public performance or music examination and have everything memorised, you will play with a much better feel. This is because you will be concentrating only on the performance. Soloing will be easier as well.

The ability to learn and memorise songs quickly is a great asset for any guitarist. Begin with the ones you think are easiest, then gradually move on to the more difficult ones.

Being able to sing the melody of a song will help you with the memorising of thousands of songs. The same thing works for solos.

If you want to improve your general memory, try reading *How to Develop a Perfect Memory* by Dominic O'Brien.

REMEMBER
Memorise the the most frequently played songs in your preferred style of music.

24

Metronome Techniques

Every serious guitarist needs to have a very good sense of musical time. If you keep losing the beat when you are playing, you are like a football player who keeps dropping the ball. After a while the team will not want you there. It is the same with a band. The better the quality of musicians you play with, the better their sense of time will be.

We are not born with a good sense of musical time, but we can develop it with a little practice each day. Every musician should own a metronome. If you haven't got one, try to get one as soon as possible. They are not very expensive. Drum machines are also good time-keeping devices, and some also have a bass or band accompaniment. The different rhythm presets are great for learning new styles. For sight-reading practice I prefer the metronome, and for improvising practice I use the drum machine.

There are different ways of setting the metronome to get a good rhythmic feel. They are:

- Rock, funk and Latin music – set the metronome to beats 1,2,3,4.
- Jazz – set the metronome to the beats 2 and 4. This gives more of a swing feel.
- Classical and reggae – set the metronome to beat on 1 and 3.
- When playing 6/8 or 12/8 time signatures I usually set the metronome to the eighth note or dotted quarter note.

Make sure you tap your foot to the beat of the metronome and after a while you will develop an inner sense of metronomic time. If you sit down to practise, the tapping leg should be the one the guitar isn't resting on, otherwise the guitar will bounce up and down making it more difficult to play.

The more advanced player can begin to experiment by playing slightly ahead of the metronome beat to give a more urgent effect. Playing slightly behind the beat gives a more laid-back effect. Practise playing in the middle of the beat, slightly ahead of the beat, then slightly behind, and feel the difference.

Always begin at a comfortable tempo. If you are making mistakes or tensing up, you are going too fast: SLOW DOWN.

When you can play a piece with no mistakes and without tensing up, move the metronome up by one notch.

Fifty to 60 beats per minute is a good tempo to begin any song or study if you are just beginning your study of the guitar. If you have not yet got a metronome, use your watch or clock if it has a second timer on it. Sixty beats per minute is one beat per second on your clock.

After you know a tune very well it is a good idea to practise it at different tempos: slow, medium and fast. Slow is approximately 50 to 100 beats per minute, medium is approximately 100 to 160 beats per minute, and fast is approximately 160 to 240 or more beats per minute. Remember to keep within your abilities; there is nothing worse than hearing someone trying to play fast who can't do it properly.

If you need to practise at quick tempos cut the metronome speed to half, and then count in cut time.

REMEMBER
Ten minutes practising with a metronome each day will improve your timing unbelievably.

25

Look After Your Body

Your body is subjected to some strenuous demands when you are practising, which can result in pain or fatigue. Here are a few tips to keep your body, mind and hands in top shape.

First of all, always sit with your back straight; there is a tendency for guitarists to lean over their instruments, which can result in painful and rounded shoulders, as well as sore back muscles. Never play with your fretting arm or elbow resting on your leg. This not only makes playing difficult, but will also make your shoulders and back sore. Having the right size chair and a footstool can help. When you are seated, your feet should touch the floor comfortably and your back should rest on the back of the chair comfortably.

Take short breaks; get out of the chair and stretch every now and then. This keeps the parts of the body that don't contribute to guitar playing active, and the short breaks help keep your mind on the job. If your mind starts wandering or thinking about what you are going to do tonight, it is time to take a break.

If you feel pain in your fingers or hands, stop immediately and rest them. Begin again slowly after a few minutes. If the pain persists, wait until the next day. If it continues for days on end, see a medical practitioner.

Learning bar chords poses a problem for guitarists. Make sure you practise them for only a few minutes at a time. Change to electric guitar strings if you play an acoustic guitar and once you get used to bar chords, change back to acoustic guitar strings. Slowly increase the time once you get used to them. When it comes time to play your first songs with them, play a few bars, then rest a few, play a few more, then rest a few more, and so on.

If you are new to playing gigs, it is a good idea to play the songs that you will be performing one after the other like a mock performance, so that you can build your endurance.

If you carry heavy equipment to the gig, wear protective gloves and use a two-wheeled handcart. When lifting, always keep a straight back.

Before performing or practising it is a good idea to warm your hands and fingers up with some scales or arpeggios. Always begin slowly. If you are going to a lesson, jam session or gig on a cold night, wear gloves to keep your hands warm. Your fingers do not perform well when they are cold.

Playing contact sports can be a problem if you are jamming or performing on a regular basis. If you play a sport where you can be injured easily, think about what is most important to you, music or sport.

If you are temporarily out of action due to injury, there are still plenty of things that you can practise, such as ear-training, theory, reading, listening, or even networking.

REMEMBER
If you look after your body, you won't have to miss practising or those special gigs or jam sessions.

26

Sing What You Play

After you have been playing for a while, say a year or two, it is a good idea to get into the habit of singing the songs you play. You don't have to be a good singer to do this; your voice will improve as you go along.

The benefits of doing this are immense: not only will your playing become more musical, but your singing voice will be able to stay on pitch better, whether you are singing lead or harmony vocals. You will be able to scat sing like George Benson if you want. Scat singing is just singing into a microphone the solo you are playing, and millions of guitarists of all styles do it.

A good way to begin is to sing the licks that you practise up and down the neck. Once you have become used to that, sing a complete solo. Keep singing your licks and complete solos for a few months, then you should be able to begin making up some of your own solos using the technique of hearing in your head the licks that you want to play. Try to leave a gap after each lick so you can think of what to play next.

That's how the professionals do it. Great licks or solos don't just fall out of the sky. You need to practise singing your licks and hearing them in your head.

You can sing chord progressions as well. Singing the top note of the chord you are playing as well as the rhythm will get you into the habit. Jazz and blues progressions are probably easiest to sing because the chords change more often.

REMEMBER
If you sing what you play, your guitar playing will improve dramatically.

27

Mind Practice

Travelling or being away from home for extended periods of time without your guitar creates a real problem. One way a lot of professional players get around this is with mind practice.

Mind practice is picturing in your mind what you would normally be practising. Close your eyes and visualise the fret board of your guitar, then play the song or exercise through in your mind, picturing yourself doing it. Sports people do this as well, especially high-jumpers and weightlifters. Next time you watch these sports on television, observe the athletes' mind practice before they start.

When you do get to your guitar, you will be physically a little rusty, but your mind will be sharp because it will know what you need to do. Mind practice can be done in aeroplanes and cars, or while you are waiting at airports, bus stations and the like. If you wake up in the middle of the night and want to practise, just lie in bed and do some mind practice. It does seem a bit strange at first, but you will quickly get used to it.

Travel Guitars

Travel guitars are a great idea. They have a small body with a normal neck, and can fit into a suitcase easily (make sure you pack yours in the middle of your clothes). If you are flying, take your travel guitar on the aeroplane as hand luggage if you need to. There are a lot of different models of travel guitar available, so check out your local music store.

REMEMBER
You can still practice without a guitar.

28

What is Improvisation?

Musical improvisation is the art of making things up as you go along, not only in the solos, but in the other parts of a song as well. Improvisation means the automatic or natural reorganisation of things that we already know. In other words, musical ideas do not just appear in somebody's head and people are not born with them; they come from ideas already stored in our memory. These musical ideas are normally called licks.

The human memory is just like a computer. Before you can use your computer, you have to store some programs in it or nothing comes out. If there are no ideas in your memory, nothing will come out either. The idea is to collect and memorise many licks.

Improvisation can be likened to learning a language. We begin by copying our parents' speech exactly. Later we learn more words and add them to our vocabulary. We can then begin to speak in a freer or more improvised way. When we are adults our spoken and written language can become quite complicated. Although two people might know the same number of words, the spontaneous reorganisation of them in different ways gives us a unique personality. This is improvisation in speech or writing.

Learning musical improvisation is the same process. We begin by copying our favourite artists. Then we add more licks to our musical vocabulary, so we can improvise more freely and expressively. After we have been doing this process for a number of years, we begin to develop a unique musical personality. Our improvisations become more complicated and we become masters, just like many others who have followed the same process.

You only need to learn licks one at a time, and you only need about twelve to twenty licks to be able to play a great solo (just like you only need twelve words to make a sentence). By rearranging these twelve to twenty licks in different orders you should be able to come up with many great-sounding improvised solos. If you learn two or three licks a week for one year, you will have between a hundred and a hundred and fifty licks – more than you need to play your first gig or jam session.

The trouble with just learning scales, not licks, is that you can sound too 'scaly' and amateurish with your improvising. The best thing about learning licks is that you will immediately sound professional. If you know that a certain lick sounds good over a certain chord, you do not have to know why; the theory can come later.

The only way to have many musical ideas and licks in your vocabulary is by repetition. You have to practise them until you can play them without thinking. When you are improvising, all the ideas you have memorised will come out, even the ones that you learnt many months or years earlier.

When studying and learning other people's improvisations or solos, it pays to learn the whole solo, not just the licks. If you learn the whole solo you will learn how the great artists build their solos up to a peak and then release to the finish. This peaking and releasing is something many guitarists find very difficult to do.

Now that you know what improvisation is, it is time to think about how to go about learning more licks.

REMEMBER
Improvisation is the spontaneous reorganisation of ideas.

29

Tips for Learning Licks

Licks are like musical words; we go from one lick to another to create musical sentences. The more licks you know, the better off you will be.

- Begin by collecting licks. You can find them in music magazines and books, learn or transcribe them from your favourite CDs, or trade them with friends. Collect licks in all styles. If you listen carefully you will hear your favourite players playing many different styles of licks. For example, the metal players play a lot of classical-type licks, the blues guitarists play a lot of jazz-type licks, etc.

- Collate your licks in a book that you can practise from. Listing them under different categories is helpful, for example blues, jazz, metal, rock, ii–V–1, etc.

- Try to relate the lick you are playing, to a chord that is in the same area of the guitar. This way, when the chord comes around in the song, you will automatically think of the various licks associated with it.

- When practising, play licks up and down the guitar neck in half-steps or one fret at a time. If you have a chord associated with the lick, play the chord first, then the lick, for better memorisation.

- Transpose the lick to different string groups. If the lick you have is played on strings one and two, play it on strings two and three, then three and four, and so on.

- Change the lick to include hammer-ons or pull-offs. Quite often when you change the string group this is made easy. If the lick has a lot of hammer-ons or pull-offs, what will it sound like if you pick every note?

- Sing all the licks as you play them. After a while you will be able to sing a solo in your head, then play it.

- Put new ideas and licks into your playing immediately, don't wait.

- Don't be afraid to copy someone else's licks. Eric Clapton, Keith Richards, Mark Knopfler, and many others have made careers out of it. Even the classical players hundreds of years ago did it. It is the quickest way to sound like a true professional. After a while the licks you know will change, and you will create your own.

- Combine a two-bar eighth-note lick, convert it to sixteenth notes, and you have a double-time jazz lick.

- Learn the licks in different octaves, and play them with different rhythms.

- If you have a C major lick, it can be made to fit over a C dominant chord by simply lowering the seventh degree if it is present, or lowering the third and seventh to fit over a C minor chord. If you lower the third, fifth, and the flatted seventh degree, it will then fit over a C diminished chord.

There are a lot of transposable-type licks – here are a few. Let your ear be the guide as some licks just don't transpose easily.

Two – five – one jazz licks can be played over other chords. The minor licks can be played over the dominant chord, and the dominant lick can be played over the minor chord.
Minor pentatonic licks can be played down three semitones, or three frets to give you a country or major sound. Major sounding licks can be played up three frets to give a bluesy sound.
Any C major lick can go over any chord in the key of C (the chords in the key of C major are; C, Dmi, Emi, F, G7, Ami, Bmi7b5) as well as D13, F#mi7b5, D7sus, and B7alt.
Any Dmi lick can fit over any chord in the key of C major, and C#7alt.
Any unaltered G7 lick can fit over any chord in the key of C major, and C#7alt.
Any C diminished lick will go over Eb dim, F# dim, Adim, B7b9, D7b9, F7b9, and Ab7b9.
Any C+ lick will fit over D+, E+, F#+, G#+, A#+.

REMEMBER
You have to learn to imitate, then assimilate, before you can innovate.

30
Transcribing

Transcribing is the art of listening to music, then writing it down on paper. At first it seems difficult, but it gets easier as you progress. Before you begin transcribing, you need at least a little knowledge of music theory, maybe to grade one or a first-level book. A good knowledge of chords, scales and ear-training is also a big help.

Equipment for Transcribing

Before you begin, you need a good pencil, a sharpener, a rubber, a ruler, and some manuscript paper – that is, paper with the music staff written on it. Never use a pen unless you are really confident in your abilities, or are doing a final copy. If you are a jazz guitarist, having a set of the chord changes from a good fake book will save a lot of time.

A must-have for transcription is a slow-down recorder that is, one that slows the music down to at least half-speed. Many these days have seven or eight different speeds, and keep the music at the same pitch. These are great for transcribing and then playing along, gradually working up the speed until you can play at the recorded tempo.

You can also get slow-down programs for your computer. These are only useful if your computer is close to your musical equipment. Also available are machines with high and low pass filters. These will cut out the high or low end, allowing you to hear more of the guitar track.

I also use a normal-speed tape deck or CD player. I find it is better for checking dynamics and articulation, rhythms, and the pitch if the range is low or hard to hear at a slower speed. I only use the slow-down recorder for the fast or difficult-to-hear passages.

Beginning to Transcribe

There are a lot of benefits in learning how to transcribe, like sight-reading improvement and learning more about different types of music, licks and the songwriting process. You will be amazed at your personal development if you spend a <u>few minutes</u> each day transcribing.

It pays to begin with something that you think will be easy. If you are not sure, ask your teacher or a more competent friend. Just writing out chord charts is a good start. When you feel comfortable with that, you can progress to writing out solos.

Hints for transcribing:

- Note the time signature, and key signature
- Beware of the first note or chord – it might not begin on beat one.
- Separate the different sections with double-bar lines.
- Work only on one bar at a time.
- Transcribe for only short periods of time; you can get tired very quickly doing this.

More points to consider:

- Play the root notes of the chords. It is very easy to think a C chord is an A minor, or vice versa. Then work out if the chords are major, minor, dominant seven or whatever.

- Write the song out in full until the end of the first chorus, then look for where you can use repeat signs, DC and DS signs and the like.

- If you are transcribing solos, write in the notes for each bar, then go back and write in the rhythms. Some people like to write the rhythms in first. That is fine if it works for you.

- When working out the rhythms, it is helpful to use a tapping foot as a reference. On very complicated passages, I like to wave my pencil in the air like the conductor of an orchestra.

- It is helpful to sing what you are going to write. It is amazing how quickly you can work out a passage if you sing it first.

- Never ever throw away your written work. I used to trash my transcriptions when I had memorised them. Ten years later, when I couldn't remember them, I had to write them out again. There are a lot of remakes in the Top 40 these days, so those old songs you have in the closet will definitely come in handy one day.

- Later on, why not have a go at transcribing the parts for other instruments? I have written out piano, drum, bass, and horn parts in the past and learnt a lot from doing so.

Transcribing is how the early pioneers of guitar learnt their craft, because in those days there weren't many books or good teachers around to speed up the learning process. Bruce Forman, the great jazz guitarist, said at a seminar that he learnt most of what he knows by spending a lot of time transcribing.

REMEMBER
A few minutes a day transcribing will be of great benefit to you.

31

A Sample Practice Schedule

Your teacher should give you give a practice schedule to adhere to. If for some reason he or she hasn't, here are a few examples.

Learners

Some good books to begin with would be *Ernie Ball Phase One and Two*, *Hal Leonard Guitar Method Book One* by W. Schmid, or *The Guitar Phase One* by W. Leavitt. Choose one of these methods to get started.

Beginner's Practice Schedule

10–15 minutes chords – review
10–15 minutes single note reading – review
10–15 minutes new work
10–15 minutes learning and playing songs
Increase or decrease the amount of time you spend on each section according to the time you have available for practice.

Take one page and make that your new work for the week. If that is too much, take half a page. Next week do the same, but make last week's work this week's review. When you are reviewing, start at the beginning of the book and play through to where you are up to with your new work. This could take a few days to get through, as you will play for the 10–15 minutes of review time. The next day you will carry on from where you left off. When you get to where your new work is, go back to the beginning and start again. This circular reviewing of your work will prevent you getting bored as you will be playing different things all the time. Once you think you know the early pieces really well, drop them from the schedule.

Intermediate

A good technique book at this level is *Modern Method for Guitar Book One* by W. Leavitt. Other suitable books are *Hal Leonard Lead Rock Method* by Al Clauson, or any other method on jazz, blues or other styles.

Take one page each week and review the previous week's work as

Intermediate Level Practice Schedule

15 minutes *Modern Method for Guitar Book One* — review
15 minutes *Lead Rock* or other improvising book — review
15 minutes new work
15 minutes learning and playing songs
15 minutes alternating theory, ear-training, listening, reading, etc.

described in the Learner's section above.

Advanced

By now you will know what works for you. Tailor a schedule for yourself, including most of the following. If you can't do all the things listed in one day, spread them over two.

Advanced Level Practice Schedule

30 minutes *Modern Method for Guitar Book 2 or 3* reviewing
30 minutes improvising, learning solos and licks
15 minutes new work
15 minutes sight-reading
15 minutes rhythm guitar
15 minutes alternating theory and listening
15 minutes ear-training
15 minutes transcribing songs and solos
15 minutes alternating other areas like piano, bass guitar, fingerstyle, etc.

REMEMBER
Having a practice schedule is like being on a diet. It is easy to plan, but difficult to stick to. Stick to yours, and success will come your way.

PERFORMING

32

Attitudes

Having the right attitude towards what you are doing is really important for guitarists. Sports people spend a lot of time working on their attitude. They fine-tune it and keep it focused, and so should we. I have seen so many players' dreams destroyed because of poor attitude. However, most musicians at the top are easy to work with and have a good attitude.

After a while most guitarists forget why they began playing. It was normally because playing was fun. After a few years of constant practice and performing, guitar-playing can begin to feel like a job, but it is only how you think of it that makes it this way. You need to keep a positive attitude, and keep remembering why it was that you began in the first place.

- Always try and look as if you are having fun, even when things are not going well. It might save the performance. Most listeners listen with their eyes. If it looks as if you are having fun, your listeners will have fun too.

- Compete with yourself if you must compete with anyone. Music is not a race; there are no winners or losers. Music is an art; different people like different things. There is always an audience for your music, no matter how good or bad you think it is.

- Always play to the best of your ability, even when you are practising. You never know who is listening. You never know who is in the audience, either; it could be someone who can provide you with a step up in the business. Some of my biggest breaks have come this way, when I least expected them.

- Keep looking for ways to improve your abilities and attitude. A good teacher or mentor can help you here. If you look under the self-improvement section in any bookstore or library you will find material on attitude improvement.

- If you think you know everything, you are in big trouble. There is just too much to learn. We are all students; some are just more advanced than others. Many of my students have told me that the more they learn, the more they realise they don't know.

- Don't be concerned about your present level of playing. Your favourite guitarist was at this level once. If you have the desire and the will to practise according to the guidelines in this book, you will progress to heights you thought unobtainable.

- Sometimes you will feel your progress is slow or even at a standstill, especially if you are working on something difficult. Don't worry. When you least expect it, you will break through. You will often feel as if you have hit a brick wall. If you keep going you will learn to overcome very difficult times in your musical life. This attitude will spill over to your daily life and will help you there as well.

- Don't compare yourself to others. There will always be someone who you think is better than you are, or who knows more. Why not try to be different?

- When I was beginning there were a few more advanced players in town who used to tease and rubbish me. They made my life a misery. It just inspired me to work harder, which I did. Years later, when I was touring with the world's best artists, some of those people asked me how I did it. I believe a positive attitude is crucial to success. How can you improve yours?

- Never let your ego get the better of you. Selfishness and inflated egos are the number-one killers of most bands or jam sessions.

A student of mine from years ago used to come for his lessons and regularly say the same thing. "If I don't do my practice everyday religiously, someone else will. That someone will live *my* dream of being a great guitarist." Today he is a professional player with two albums to his credit. It was his attitude that made the difference.

REMEMBER
Your attitude determines your altitude.

33
Confidence

There is no doubt about it, you can tell a confident guitarist a mile away. Many people have asked me over the years, "How do I become a super-confident player?" I could write a book on this subject alone. Here I will discuss just the main points.

There are two types of confidence: confidence in your ability, and performing confidence.

Confidence in Your Ability

Confidence in your ability comes from knowing you can perform the feats you set out to do. You spend many hours practising the music you are going to play, and then you keep within those limits. You know you can play your material without fault, and you know how to cover up if you do make a mistake.

Most people have not learnt how to be confident when mistakes happen. But you can prepare for this. When you make a mistake that throws you, try to keep counting the time. Begin playing again at beat one of the next bar. After a while you will get used to it. When you can do this, try to forget the mistake you have just made and come in on the very next note. Even the professionals make mistakes! The reason you can't hear them is because they can cover them up well.

You are likely to feel anxious when you are under-prepared, or going outside your limits. That is why it is important to practise regularly. Learning as much as possible in your chosen area will increase the limits to which you can play confidently, without fear.

Most guitarists experience some self-doubt at some stage. This is only natural, but you have to learn not to worry about what others think and just get on with the job at hand.

Performing Confidence

Performing confidence is something people have a lot of trouble with. Here are some ways of developing your confidence in front of other people:

- Perform as often as you can. If you are new to performing, get some friends together and play for them. Start with just a few songs; as you become more self-assured you can increase the amount of time you perform. Most people tend to tense up when they begin performing, which hinders their ability to play well. By performing on a regular basis you will learn to relax, making for better performances.

- Don't be concerned if you get butterflies in your stomach before you perform. Even professional performers get a few butterflies before they go on stage. After a while you learn how to convert this nervous energy into positive energy, and it will help you perform better.

- Tape yourself playing every day, then play it back and critique yourself. It is surprising how many people freak out when the red recording light goes on, so doing this will definitely help your confidence in a recording studio as well.

- Find people to perform for at your church, school, workplace or music society. Also look on music store noticeboards. Always carry your guitar with you; you will be surprised how many opportunities there will be for you to perform.

You could be the best player in the world in your practice room, but if you don't get out and perform, you won't build your confidence enough to become a great player. The best guitarists have a lot of confidence in their ability. Always bear in mind, though, that confidence in your ability doesn't mean showing off or having an inflated ego.

REMEMBER
Always be ready and willing when an opportunity to perform comes your way.

34

Getting More Gigs

People often ask me how they can get more gigs. Apart from getting yourself known in the musical community, the answer is to learn more styles. If you are a rock player, learn some jazz and country? The more styles you know, the greater the range of gigs that will come your way. It takes a little more discipline but is worth it. If you specialise in just one style you are really limiting yourself, especially when the style of the moment changes. If Latin suddenly became the style of the moment, would you be ready to cash in?

One of the best ideas I know is to practise bass line and chord accompaniment. Once you are good at this you will be able to do gigs with just yourself and a singer, sax or other horn player, and simply adding a drum machine will make you sound like a band. People I know who play in this style are very busy, and making good money. *Big Ax* volumes 1 and 2, by Jack Grassel will help with this style.

Another worthwhile idea is to study piano arrangements. A lot of gigs don't use a piano, but if you can play in that style the telephone won't stop ringing. Studying how to play with a pianist is also a good idea. You have to think in a totally different way, because if you both play the same thing, it doesn't sound very good. Some funky single picking lines sound good in these situations, or just not playing anything for a while, otherwise called "laying out".

Chord melody in either a jazz or classical guitar style is an area which can provide a lot of work. These types of players tend to work the restaurants and smaller venues, weddings and parties, as well as business promotions.

Improving your reading ability will definitely pay off. This will mean you'll be able to work in the backing bands of well-known artists, do stage shows, television and recording dates and all sorts of other gigs where reading is required. Reading gigs are normally more highly paid, and in better venues.

The more gigs that come your way, the faster you improve. Gigs are like getting paid to practise. The more of them that you do the better off you will be financially and personally. You do not need to be an advanced-level player to be out gigging or even busking. How much do you currently get paid to practise?

 REMEMBER
Increasing your range of abilities will improve your earning capacity as a musician.

35
Performance Preparation

Everybody who performs has different views on how to prepare. These are some of my thoughts:

- Make sure you know the music well. It should be learnt well ahead of the performance, not on the day. If you are doing a reading gig, however, you probably won't get a chance to see the music until you are there.

- If I am the one picking the songs for the concert, I begin with easier ones, save the difficult ones for the middle, and leave a few more easy ones for the end.

- If it is a night concert, take a walk in the afternoon to help you relax. If you think you can relax by taking alcohol or any other drug, forget it. It normally ruins your performance as well as your reputation.

- Make a habit of turning up at least one hour before the show so you can warm up, test your gear, and just relax. You won't perform well when under stress or in a rush.

- Don't eat a large meal close to the performance or you will feel drowsy.

- Don't practise a lot on the day of the performance. A light practice session sometime during the day works well; practise the difficult parts of the performance.

- If you are travelling to the gig in cold weather, wear a good pair of gloves so your fingers remain warm. Cold fingers do not perform very well.

- Here is a breathing technique I teach my students that will help overcome undue nervousness. Breathe in slowly to a count of four, hold the breath for four counts, then slowly breathe out for four counts. Do this about three or four times and you will feel relaxed, and maybe even experience a high. When you have got used to this technique, you will be able to do it between songs if you need to.

- Always try to play musically. You will be remembered for your musical abilities rather than your showing-off abilities. The only competition there is in music is the one with yourself – to improve.

- Always play to the best of your ability and within your capabilities. You never know who is listening.

- If the local guitar guru or even Eric Clapton turns up to hear you play, don't be too concerned. In my experience the guru will introduce him or herself, and become a good friend. If Eric Clapton happens to turn up at one of your concerts, then think yourself lucky and go and tell all your friends.

REMEMBER
Proper preparation makes for a good performance.

MISCELLANEOUS

36
Examinations

Wherever there are music schools or music teachers, there are normally opportunities to enter examinations.

Preparing for examinations is a positive experience for most people, and a boost to their personal motivation. If you are thinking about entering tertiary-level music courses you will have to have passed some examinations first. Most universities require proof that you can play up to some required level, normally grade eight. The theory level required is normally at least about grade five. Even if you are not going on to tertiary-level music, the certificates that you receive after each examination look good in your curriculum vitae, and are looked upon favourably by most employers.

However, many teachers and students seem to be obsessed with the examination system and there are issues there that you need to aware of. If all you are going to do is work on examination material, chances are, you will end up like a lot of classical piano players I know who only know twenty-four pieces, the three pieces per grade they did from grade one to grade eight. They are so tired of these twenty-four pieces that they don't want to play them anymore, and they don't know anything else. These types of players are victims of the obsession with examinations. They are not really good players. They have fooled themselves into thinking that certificates make good musicians.

At every grade level you should be able to play at least fifty pieces, from a range of different styles. Once you have achieved all the work required and know the fifty pieces, then and only then is it time to think about entering an examination. So the grade level you have reached should be a true reflection of the level that you have achieved. And you should easily achieve between ninety and one hundred per cent. I have seen so many grade-five players who play much better than a grade-eight player, simply because they have taken their time and learnt properly.

When studying with a good teacher you should be there to learn as much as you can and hopefully enjoy the experience. If all you want to do is pass examinations as fast as you can, all your efforts and money are going to be wasted.

One thing many people fail to realise about any examination is that if they pass grade one with a mark of seventy-five per cent, they really only know three-quarters of the subject material. When it comes time to do grade two they will have to put more work in to patch up the bits they didn't understand in grade one, or their mark will drop to maybe sixty-six per cent. Of course at grade-three level the predicted mark would come in around fifty-eight – sixty per cent, if extra work has not been done to fill in all the holes in their education.

With most examining bodies' pass mark being at around sixty per cent, you can see they are now coming within the fail range. Failing an examination has large negative psychological effects and should be avoided at all times. It is the number-one reason many people give up music or want to quit school, and all because they have forgotten or could not understand some minor concepts they had learnt earlier.

If you or your teacher do not think you can pass an examination with at least ninety per cent, it is time to review the situation.

If you are a student at a university or other tertiary institution, make a habit of learning as much as you can while you are there, not just enough to pass the tests. If you don't, I guarantee you will kick yourself later.

If you are interested in entering examinations, here are a few of the best examining bodies that private music teachers use. Write and request some information from them.

For modern guitar examinations

Australian and New Zealand
    Cultural Arts Ltd
P O Box 70
Greensborough
Vic 3088
Australia.

Trinity College London
16 Park Crescent
London
W1N4AP
UK.
http://www.trinitycollege.co.uk

For classical guitar examinations

The Associated Board of the Royal
    Schools of Music
14 Bedford Square
London
WC1B3JG
UK.
http://www.abrsm.ac.uk

The following are some university-level institutions that are popular with guitarists. There are also many more, too numerous to mention here. Check them out by looking in trade magazines or searching the World Wide Web.

Berklee College of Music
1140 Boylston St
Boston
Massachusetts 02215
USA.
http://www.berklee.com

The Musicians Institute
1655 McCadden Place
Hollywood
CA900026
USA.
http://www.mi.edu

Massey University
Private Bag 11222
Palmerston North
New Zealand.
http://www.massey.ac.nz

REMEMBER
Learning music is much more than just passing examinations.

37

Networking

Networking is all about making and keeping many musical friends – not just guitar players but all types of musicians, as well as agents, promoters, bandleaders and anyone else in the business. Because they have so much in common, musical friends can help and encourage each other. You will come across many new ideas if you hang out with other musicians.

Great conversation starters:

- I thought your playing tonight was great, thank you.
- So-and-so told me you are a guitar player, is that right?
- You had some great licks there, where did you get them?
- When is your band back in town again?
- I noticed in that last song you had an interesting sound. How did you achieve that?

Backstage

It is surprising who you can meet if you go backstage. The major rock acts normally have massive security backstage so you won't be able to get in, but other acts don't. You can meet the guitarists in bands of every other genre if you hang out backstage. They are usually only too willing to talk to you and share their experiences.

Business Cards

Always have professionally printed business cards to hand out at meetings. The more your card is distributed the better you will get known. Make sure all the agents in town have one as well. This could lead to more gigs.

Organisations and Clubs

Joining professional or trade organisations, clubs and unions for musicians will automatically increase your potential network. Regular attendance at the meetings is helpful, as is participating in the activities, serving on committees, and assuming leadership roles. Always arrive early and leave late so you can meet more people.

Voluntary Work

Volunteering to play for charity organisations is another way you can expand your network of friends. Try theatre groups, hospitals, rest homes, churches, sports clubs and the like.

Referrals

Referring people to someone you know is a good way of getting a lot of referrals back. Make sure you know the person you are referring very well first though; a bad referral can backfire.

When people first begin playing they may seem shy or aloof. It may be that they are insecure about their playing abilities. Why not introduce yourself and pay them a compliment? Both of you will benefit from the encounter. Try not to offend anybody; you never know when you might need that person's help or advice, or you might even end up playing in the same band or jam session. Don't take things too personally if someone doesn't seem too friendly. Chances are they are just having a bad day.

REMEMBER
Networking is essential for survival in the music business.

38

Moving On

When you are moving up the ladder of success from amateur to the semi-professional and professional ranks, and the telephone doesn't stop ringing because everybody wants your guitar playing skills, what do you do next?

Just as in any other business, there is always something to work on: accounting and marketing, a new project like an album or video, time management, writing new material, and many other things. These tasks can be divided into two sections: music and business. The music side of things is easy to look after. Most guitarists like this side of the business and are good at it. When it comes to the business side of things, for instance taxation, insurance, dealing with bank managers and lawyers, they often run for cover.

If you don't want to handle the business side of things you could employ a business manager to do it for you. However, most guitarists who are just beginning to work on a professional basis cannot afford that luxury. Managers normally take a ten to fifteen per cent commission, which can substantially reduce your income.

You will need a good accountant and lawyer as you progress and it would be wise to check out those in your area who specialise in the music industry. These two people will become your most important business contacts.

Your Accountant

Your accountant will look after all your taxation and other money affairs, which can start to get complicated, especially if you are going to set up a company. Good records of your business expenses will have to be kept as well, because they are deductible against your income. A first meeting with an accountant is normally free, so don't hesitate to contact one. At this meeting they will discuss such things as how to keep your records of income and outgoings. Accountants can save you a lot of money in tax alone if you use them wisely.

In most countries in the Western world, tax evasion is a criminal offence. Many musicians get caught in this trap through ignorance. Check out your tax obligations from the start.

Your Lawyer

Your lawyer can take care of all the contractual and other legal matters. The more successful you become, the more you will need a lawyer. Never, never, never sign any contract without having your lawyer read it through first, and then explain the things to you in simple language. You could be signing something you do not want. It is surprising how many beginning musicians, eager to get ahead, have been ripped off in this way.

Business Procedure

A good knowledge of business procedure is a must. Learning how to deal with business people and procedures is just like learning how to play the guitar: the more you do it, the better you get at it. Like music theory, it pays to know what you are doing and why.

If you are not very good at the negotiating process, it is a good idea to have an agent who can negotiate the gigs for you. Most of the time guitarists work too cheaply. Agents can command a higher fee for your work, making their commission a worthwhile investment.

There are many books and courses on small businesses. If you want to do a small-business course, look in the yellow pages of the local telephone directory or contact your local commerce centre. It is always a good idea to read many books on the subject, so you can get different views. After reading them, put some of the ideas into practice; if they don't work for you, change them. Buy your own copies of the best books, so that you can use them as a reference should the need arise. You need books that cover negotiating, selling, telephone skills, marketing, contracts, dealing with difficult people, and anything else that will help you to better your business skills.

Never, ever, sell any songs, lyrics or other items that you have written. There is a story that Benny King sold the song "Stand by Me" for twenty-five dollars, because he had no money for food. The song went on to become a best seller many times over for its new owner.

Time management is a must if you are going to have any time left to practice, especially if you still have a day job. It's easy to spend all day negotiating gigs, selling albums, talking to your lawyer about contracts, contacting radio stations, travelling from gig to gig and so on. Soon there is no time left for what you like doing most, playing the guitar. So make a big effort to become an efficient time manager. There are many good books available on this subject.

Networking is essential if you want to make it big. It pays to have contacts who are amateurs, as well as some who are professionals in the business. When you begin to travel the world – as most good musicians do – you begin to realise how small the musical community is, and how important it is to have a good network. Again, there are many good books available on this topic.

It is at this stage that you will want to check out more advanced teachers, especially if you are still with your first teacher. You need some new challenges, and you need to get out of your comfort zone. You could do some master classes overseas, with some of the big names in the guitar world. Teachers of advanced students are normally only found in the large cities, and booking a time with them can be difficult, so call them early to ensure your place. At this level it is absolutely essential that you are positive and self-motivated. Re-read the chapter on motivation, and as many books on the subject as possible.

By now you should have acquired or be in the process of acquiring the following equipment: a cellphone, a fax machine, a website, and an e-mail address for instant communication with your contacts. On the music side, you should have professional-model guitars, amplifiers, cords and effects if you use them. A reliable car or van for transporting your equipment from gig to gig is also high on the list. Do not rely on borrowing equipment from your friends. Sometimes you will not be able to borrow it when you need it, or it will be out of service just when you have an important gig to do.

Moving up the ladder of success is a wonderful feeling for anyone involved in the arts. There is no better way to make a living than doing something you love. I, personally, can't wait to get out of bed each morning so I can start work!

When beginning a professional career, it is very easy to work seven days a week and not have any time to yourself. It is essential to take breaks, to recharge your internal batteries. You might have noticed how great you feel when returning to your day job after a good holiday. It is also a good idea to have other interests outside of music like keeping fit, golf, reading and so on.

If you would rather remain an amateur player, I can tell you that many amateur guitarists are just as good as some of the world's top names. A lot of amateurs have even written songs for some of the world's top artists, and some who have had recordings do very well for themselves as well.

REMEMBER
Moving up the ladder of success requires new skills that need to be practised.

39

Books to Add to Your Collection

These are just some of the good books that are available.

Slide Guitar by Arlen Roth. New York: Oak Publications.

Fingerstyle Guitar by Ken Perlman. Milwaukee, USA: Hal Leonard Publishing, HL00000081.

For Guitar Players Only by Tommy Tedesco. USA: Dale Zdenek Publications.

Concepts (arranging for fingerstyle guitar) by Howard Morgan. Miami, USA: CPP Belwin.

The Jazz Guitarist's Handbook by Bruce Forman. San Francisco: Guitar Solo Publications.

Jazz Band Rhythm Guitar by Bruce Forman. USA: Mel Bay, MB97022.

The Advancing Guitarist by Mick Goodrick. Milwaukee, USA: Hal Leonard, HL00603009.

Jazz Conception by Jim Snidero. Germany: Advance Music.

Great Country Riffs for Guitar by Jon Chappell. New York: Cherry Lane Music.

The Charlie Parker Omnibook. New York: Atlantic Music Corp.

Nashville Guitar by Arlen Roth. New York: Oak Publications.

Country Guitar Styles by Mike Ihde. Boston, USA: Berklee Press.

Rock Guitar Styles by Mike Ihde. Boston, USA: Berklee Press.

Blues You Can Use by John Ganapes. Milwaukee, USA: Hal Leonard Publishing, HL00695007.

Latin American Guitar Guide by Rico Stover. USA: Mel Bay, MB95478BCS.

Old Time and Fiddle Tunes Vol 1 by Dix Bruce. USA: Mel Bay, MB94339BCD.

The Inner Game of Music by Barry Green & Timothy Gallwey. London: Pan Books.

How to Win Friends and Influence People by Dale Carnegie. London: Angus & Robertson Publishers.

Psycho-Cybernetics 2000 by Bobbe Sommer. New Jersey, USA: Prentice Hall.

Effortless Mastery by Kenny Werner. Indiana, USA: Jamey Aebersold Publishing.

How to Write a Hit Song by Molly-Ann Leiken. Milwaukee, USA: Hal Leonard Publishing, HL00330006.

Managing Lyric Structure by Pat Pattison. Boston, USA: Berklee Press.

The Songwriters Rhyming Dictionary by Sammy Cahn. USA: Facts on File Publications. ISBN 0-285-62637-X.

Making the Ultimate Demo by Micheal Molenda. Milwaukee, USA: Hal Leonard Publishing, HL00330071.

Jazz Savophone Licks, Phrases and Patterns by Arnie Berle. USA: Mel Bay. MB 94329.

How to Create and Develop a Jazz Sax Solo by Arnie Berle. USA: Mel Bay MB 94528.

All Blues for Jazz Guitar by Jim Fergusson. USA: Mel Bay. MB 06842 BCD.

Any books written by the following authors: Joe Pass, Barry Galbraith, William Leavitt, Howard Roberts, George van Eps, Ted Green and Mickey Baker and Jerry Bergonzi, David Baker, Jerry Cocker.

40
Publishers

The following are some of the world's leading music publishers. There are many others. Write to them for a catalogue, or look them up on the World Wide Web. Most of the books mentioned in this publication can be purchased from these publishers.

Alfred Publishing
P O Box 10393
Van Nuys
CA91410
USA
http://www.pjballantine.com

Mel Bay
#4 Industrial Drive
Pacific
MO 63069-0066
USA
http://www.melbay.com

Jamey Aebersold Jazz
P O Box 1244
New Albany
IN 47151-1244
USA
http://www.jazzbooks.com

Music Dispatch
P O Box 13920
Milwaukee
WI 53213
USA
http://www.musicdispatch.com

Hot Licks
P O Box 337
Pound Ridge
NY 10576
USA
http://www.hotlicks.com

Sher Music
P O Box 445
Petaluma
CA 94953
USA
http://www.shermusic.com

 REMEMBER
Keep a current catalogue handy so you know which new books are available.

Afterword

I have tried to keep the many ideas contained in this book simple. I suggest you read it through every few months to gain new ways of improving the quality of your practice. The ways you think and practise are keys to success or failure. By following the advice in this book you can be assured that you will be on the right track, and that you will be as successful as you can be.

I wrote this book because so many teachers and students ask how I consistently turn out the best guitarists Downunder. It is only on rare occasions that my exam students do not receive a distinction or honours pass mark. Those who go on to join the professional ranks are in hot demand because they are well-rounded professionals who can read, improvise, play all styles, and have a good manner both personally and in business.

The ideas contained in this book have been gathered over many years of practising and performing. As far as I am aware there is no other book on the commercial market which discusses the practice habits of professional or highly successful guitarists. There are many general practice books, but they are not written specifically for the guitar. Many of the world's top guitarists tend to keep their ideas and routines secret. If you follow all the ideas in this book, and take your time doing them, you can be a highly sought-after guitarist.

I would appreciate any ideas you may have as a result of reading this book and applying the techniques outlined. My contact address is included on the last page.

One final bit of advice: **NEVER, NEVER, NEVER GIVE UP!**

Bibliography

Big Ax, Frozen Sky Records, Wisconsin, USA.
Classic Guitar Technique, Franco Colombo Publications, New York.
Ernie Ball Book One, Ernie Ball Publishing, USA.
Ernie Ball Phase One, Ernie Ball Publishing, USA.
Ernie Ball Phase Two, Ernie Ball Publishing, USA.
For Guitar Players Only, Dale Zdenek Publications, USA.
Gibson Electrics, Hal Leonard Publishing, HL00704488, USA.
Guitar Comping, Weybridge Productions, Vermont, USA.
Hal Leonard Guitar Method Book One, Hal Leonard Publishing, USA.
Hal Leonard Lead Rock Method, Hal Leonard Publishing, HL00699043, USA.
How to Develop a Perfect Memory, Pavilion Books, London.
How to Learn Tunes, Jamey Aebersold Publishing, Indiana, USA.
Howard Roberts Guitar Manual, Playback Music Publishing, Hollywood, USA.
Improve Exam Results in 30 Days, Thorsons, USA.
Jamey Aebersold Jazz Ear Training Course, Jamey Aebersold Publishing,
    Indiana, USA.
Jazz Conception, Advance Music, Germany.
Master Your Theory, EMI Publishing, Australia.
Mel Bay Book One, Mel Bay Publishing, USA.
Mel Bay's Modern Guitar Method Grade One, Mel Bay Publishing, USA.
Melodic Rhythms for Guitar, Berklee Press, Boston, USA.
Modern Method for Guitar, Berklee Press, Hal Leonard Publishing,
    HL50449400.
Modern Recording Techniques, by Huber & Runstein, USA.
Psycho Cybernetics 2000, Prentice Hall, Englewood Cliffs, New Jersey, USA.
Reading Contemporary Guitar Rhythms, Berklee Press, Boston, USA.
Reading Key Jazz Rhythms, Advance Music, Germany.
Solo Guitar Playing, Collier Books, New York.
The Fender Stratocaster, Hal Leonard Publishing, 00183682, USA.
The Grove Dictionary of Jazz, Macmillan Press, London.
The Grove Dictionary of Music, Macmillan Press, London.
The Guitar Handbook, Pan Books, London.
The Guitar Phase One, Berklee Press, Boston, USA.
The Jazz Language, Studio 224, Miami, USA.
The New Grove Gospel, Blues and Jazz, Macmillan Press, London.
The Oxford Companion to Music, Oxford University Press, Oxford.

About the Author

Kevin Downing has been a professional guitarist most of his working life. He has performed with some of the world's biggest names in the entertainment industry, and has appeared on many television and radio shows. His students are among the best players in Australasia. They travel from all over New Zealand to study with him.

Kevin is available for performances and seminars by contacting the address below.

P.O. Box 4586
Palmerston North
New Zealand. 5315
e-mail kevin@guitar.co.nz
Web site http://www.guitar.co.nz